DICK TRACY

THE MAKING OF THE MOVIE

by

Mike Bonifer

A
BANTAM
TRADE
PAPERBACK

®

BANTAM BOOKS

New York • Toronto • London • Sydney • Auckland

DICK TRACY: THE MAKING OF THE MOVIE
A Bantam Book / June 1990

Cover photo courtesy of The Walt Disney Company.

The book was designed and the project supervised by Michael Mendelsohn and
Patricia Ollague of M 'N O Production Services, Inc.

ISBN 0-553-34900-7

Published simultaneously in the United States and Canada

Bantam Books are published by Bantam Books, a division of Bantam Doubleday Dell Publishing
Group, Inc. Its trademark, consisting of the words "Bantam Books" and the portrayal of a
rooster, is Registered in U.S. Patent and Trademark Office and in other countries, Marca
Registrada. Bantam Books, 666 Fifth Avenue, New York, New York 10103

PRINTED IN THE UNITED STATES OF AMERICA

0 9 8 7 6 5 4 3 2 1

For Adam and Alex

Acknowledgements

The inimitable Howard Green of Walt Disney Pictures has my permanent gratitude. Disney's Michael Lynton, Greg Cosby, Robyn Tynan, Jeanette Steiner, Louise Spencer, Terry Press, Jim Lefkowitz, and Hilary Clark all pitched in. Carol Kim and Victor Bazaz of Mulholland Productions came through time and again. The Man in the Midwest, L. G. Weaver, delivered his usual punch. The Man in Mid-Air, Tim Onosko, gave directions. Glenn Campbell of Buena Vista Visual Effects provided much of the information on—what else?—Visual Effects. Warner Bros. Records' Liz Rosenberg did her bit, as did Donna Drexler and George Bamber. David Moritz clipped the diopter shots. Larry Doucet contributed photos from his incredible collection of Dick Tracy memorabilia. Janet, my wife, with her unerring eye for design, helped me edit them. Thanks also to Lou Aronica and Robert Simpson of Bantam. And to the many who are quoted in the book, thanks for the interviews. It was an education.

Contents

DICK TRACY ON FILM
and
"Calling Dick Tracy! Calling Dick Tracy!"
or
TRACY GETS CHANGE OF VENUE

Dick Tracy on Film—now there's a concept.

It works for a movie studio like Jeffrey Katzenberg's Disney/Touchstone, which relied on the huge audience generated by more than fifty years of Chester Gould's comic strip creation to springboard DICK TRACY into the box-office spotlight.

It works for moviegoers, who want their heroes larger than life and their villains hissably bad, who want to see Virtue triumph over Vice, and True Love conquer all.

And especially, it works for the people who made the movie.

Dick Tracy on Film. The filmmakers said it to themselves, and to one another, in so many different ways that, like an oft-repeated mantra, this simple idea took them to a new level of creative consciousness, where they were able to make the connections that electrified the motion picture.

Getting Dick Tracy on film became Warren Beatty's personal mission. Beatty sought a breakthrough motion picture that would fuse the functions of Writing, Production Design, Costuming, Photography, Acting, Editing, Music, and Visual Effects into a focused whole. It ended up being an awesome challenge: Could every frame of the film contain in it the genetic code of the entire film? Could he unify and control the hundreds of energies at work on the production of his movie by channeling them into this four-word formula? Dick Tracy on Film. It seem simple enough. But then, so did $E=mc^2$. The implications, in both cases, were profound.

Chester Gould's Dick Tracy, as he appeared in the 1930s.

Warren Beatty's Dick Tracy.

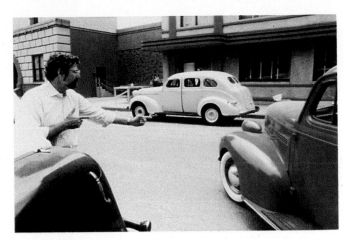

Executive producer Barrie Osborne (in white shirt) and stunt supervisor Bill Burton laid out the action for the final shootout using Polaroid photos and themselves as stand-ins.

Surrounded by his production team, Beatty the Director watches Beatty the Actor perform in a video playback of one of the film's scenes.

Flattop, after wiping out the card game Rubout. Flattop attacks the cardplayers.

Dick Tracy is a film about colors. From Tracy's sunlight-yellow to the dead-black of the underworld night, the colors of the film are its language. They charge and enliven its drama, its action, its love. In *Dick Tracy,* color and emotion interlock in a storytelling chemistry just as complex as strands of DNA. When Madonna sings . . . the Stephen Sondheim song, the Richard Sylbert set design, the Vittorio Storaro lighting, and the Milena Canonero dress all work in harmony to color the character of Breathless Mahoney. When Big Boy rampages . . . everything in his path gets swept into the reddish hell of his wickedness.

The people involved in making *Dick Tracy* have together been nominated for sixty-three Academy Awards. Beatty himself is the only person ever to be nominated in four different categories on two separate occasions—for *Heaven Can Wait* and *Reds.* Movies don't get any more pedigreed than this. Yet, it's safe to say that Warren Beatty and every one of his collaborators were venturing into virgin territory. Never had a movie been made using the conventions of comic-strip art in this manner to tell a story. The experience was new to all of them, and they were determined to make it just as new for movie audiences.

Madonna strikes a Breathless pose.

Chester Gould at work on a Tracy strip in his Chicago Tribune office in the 1960s.

The comic-strip conventions are these: They are shot in vignette, the frame doesn't move; all colors are primary, as are emotions; staging is simple and perfectly designed; and they are by definition comic—high-spirited detours around reality. With these, as well as a few nuances particular to Chester Gould's Dick Tracy comics as their touchstones, the filmmakers traveled an arduous and interesting path to create the finished film.

This book documents their journey. More accurately, it documents the descriptions and accounts of the people who blazed the trail: Warren Beatty,

Madonna, production designer Richard Sylbert, costume designer Milena Canonero, director of photography Vittorio Storaro, makeup artists John Caglione and Doug Drexler, visual effects supervisors Michael Lloyd and Harrison Ellenshaw, executive producer Barrie Osborne, production manager Jon Landau, and editor Richard Marks.

"If you ever look at the Chester Gould comic strip, he would not call a prison Alcat*raz*, he would call it Alcaratz," noted Jon Landau, *Dick Tracy*'s production manager/co-producer. It was the type of thing that told the production team how far off-center to take the

movie. Just an anagram's worth, just a tad tilted—
enough to keep the audience giddy with double takes
and small surprises. Every scene, indeed every *shot*,
became a moment. A yellow car on a yellow street and
a man in a yellow raincoat. Madonna sings Sondheim.
Newspapers whirl. Flattop kills as Big Boy cackles. The
Kid knows too much. A two-way wrist radio. The boiler
explodes. A matte. A miniature. A gag, a punch, a
kiss. . . . The stuff of movies, humming at a frequency no
film fan ever felt before.

The diopter shots did it for editor Richard Marks,
who has cut such noteworthy films as *Broadcast News*
and *Terms of Endearment*. A diopter is a split-focus
lens, which permits two images in the same frame—
one close-up and one long-shot—in focus at the same
time. "The diopter shots are remarkable, and for me
define the style of this picture," remarked Marks. He
described a shot of the Kid staring at Dick Tracy's wrist
radio from across a table as typical of the Hitchcockian
images created by the diopter. "It's fun stuff that defines a very stylized realty."

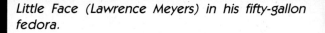

*Little Face (Lawrence Meyers) in his fifty-gallon
fedora.*

It is not any one effect in itself, but all the production
values together expressed in a new language, that
translate into Dick Tracy on Film. "It's not a building with
green windows that makes a comic book," pointed out
Jon Landau. "It's that same building with a Flattop character walking out of it, getting into the biggest, bluest
limousine you've ever seen, and driving off on a red
street into a matte painting. *That's* a comic book!"

The comic strip that inspired the movie began in the
Chicago Tribune—N.Y. News Syndicate in October of

1931 at the hand of Chester Gould, a native of Pawnee, Oklahoma, who had moved to Chicago ten years earlier in search of cartooning work. Those infamous ten years between 1921 and 1931 in Chicago bombarded the Oklahoman with enough raw material to keep a crimestopper occupied for life. Bootleggers, speakeasies, Thompson submachine guns, and abominable bad guys like Al Capone had the folks back in Pawnee plenty worried about young Chester.

Gould's original name for the strip was "Plainclothes Tracy," but his publisher simplified it to "Dick Tracy." The name said it all, and the strip was a hit right from the start.

Dick Tracy joined the pantheon of hard-boiled detective heroes, sorting out good from evil with a sureness of purpose that Depression-era readers found refreshing. Gould cased Chicago crime labs in his off-hours looking for ideas and authenticity. From the very first strip, when Tracy deduces by the way a "woman" ducks a punch that she's actually a man, a bizarre realism marked the detective's exploits.

A serialized radio show in the 1930s and a series of films in the 1940s added to the character's popularity, as did the merchandising of the strip. A year after Dick Tracy's introduction, promotional buttons bearing his square-jawed profile became the first in a long line of Dick Tracy memorabilia. Dolls, games, miniature police

stations, a battery of toy guns and handcuffs, comic books, storybooks, and, of course, the famous two-way wrist radio soon joined the cavalcade.

The wrist radio, always indicated by an arrow, was typical of Gould's ability to arrest his readers' attention with a gimmick that they couldn't find anywhere else in the comics. His gruesome villains also sprung from his desire to "sell" the strip to readers. Pruneface, The Brow, and The Rodent got people talking. (And evidently tapped their darker impulses, as well. When Gould killed off Flattop, readers sent flowers and staged a wake outside the *Tribune* offices.) In later years, the cartoonist added characters like B. O. and Sparkle

Tracy memorabilia from the last five decades, from the collection of L. Doucet.

Plenty to Tracy's retinue, and added magnetic coupes and air cars to his modes of transportation.

The increasingly graphic design of the strip—with the black ink blaring like one-hundred-point head-lines—urged the reader's eye from one scene to the next. Influenced by silent films and newsreels, Gould laid out the story like a movie—intercutting between locations, between long shots and close-ups, be-tween characters and inanimate objects. His business instincts—he had a commerce degree from North-western—told him that all the innovation would keep him ahead of the competition. His skills as an artist made that innovation possible.

After forty-six years of fighting crime on the funny pages, Chester Gould retired in 1977, turning the strip over to writer Max Allan Collins. Collins has since worked with two Gould assistants: Rick Fletcher (1977–1983) and Dick Locher (1983–present). Gould died in May 1985, at the age of eighty-four. His daugh-ter, Jean Gould O'Connell, visited the *Dick Tracy* set during the production of the film and, from all reports, liked what she saw.

What she saw was a movie unfolding from the pages of her father's imagination. Gould's most notorious villains had united under Big Boy's leadership for an attempt to overthrow Tracy one and for all, and run the City. The script, as fashioned by Jim Cash and Jack Epps Jr. *(Top Gun),* Bo Goldman *(Melvin and Howard),* and Beatty, opens with the Kid. He's running. Why? From what? To where? Those questions are the first domi-

Tracy goes for a ride, courtesy of Flattop and Itchy.

noes of the plot, which will eventually crisscross, double back, and overlap in a beautiful storytelling design.

Three stories intertwine throughout *Dick Tracy:* Tracy and the Kid; the love triangle of Tracy, Breathless Mahoney, and Tess Trueheart; and the confrontation between Tracy and Big Boy. Each story crystallizes into a hard choice that must be made by the hero.

Tracy must choose between the isolated life of a cop, and the responsibilities embodied by the Kid, played by nine-year-old Charlie Korsmo from Minneapolis (whose one previous film credit was *Men Don't Leave,* with Jessica Lange). Jon Landau helped conduct the nationwide search that led to Korsmo: "What Warren found most interesting in Charlie was his intellect. A nine-year-old kid who has already completed his high school math requirements." The director, said Landau, disdained rehearsals for scenes involving the Kid because "the best things you get with kids are spontaneous. You might get something great in rehearsal and not be able to get it again." Rehearsal time, as spent by Beatty, was a time for actors to get to know one another. "Charlie went up to Warren's house to watch the Super Bowl. And that goes a long way, it really does."

Glenne Headly (Tess Trueheart) and Madonna (Breathless Mahoney) force Tracy into a tug-of-war between a drive in the country with Tess and a roll in the rumble seat with Breathless. This triangle, as constructed by editor Richard Marks, "provides the emotional bedrock of the picture—the relationship between Tracy and Tess Trueheart that nothing can shake, no matter what the temptation—and that comic-strip triumph of what is right."

Tracy at home in The City.

Breathless Mahoney (Madonna) tempts Tracy to take off his hat and more.

Steve the Tramp gets a visitor. In Dick Tracy, shadows often carry as much weight as flesh-and-blood characters.

The street blazes an angry red as a yellow fireball signals Tracy's triumph.

The third strand of the storyline focuses on Tracy's battle with Big Boy Caprice, played by Al Pacino.

The casting of Pacino may be the best example of what production designer Richard Sylbert described as Beatty's "ability to wait until something better comes along." The production team had made exhaustive lists of the actors who could play Big Boy, actors who were either not quite right for the role, or who were unavailable. Time was getting short. Then Beatty saw Pacino in a restaurant one day during lunch. Pacino, who had just wrapped *Sea of Love,* hadn't been on any of the Big Boy lists, but he was the "something better" Beatty was waiting for. With the help of prosthetics designed by makeup artists Caglione and Drexler, Pacino hatched a wickedly funny Big Boy—"a cross between Hitler and Groucho Marx," declared executive producer Osborne—that perfectly counterweights Beatty's straightlaced Tracy.

Seymour Cassel and James Keane portray longtime Tracy sidekicks Sam Catchem and Pat Patton; Bill Forsythe is Flattop; Mandy Patinkin tickles the ivories and sings for the first time on film as 88 Keys; R. G. Armstrong appears as Pruneface; Ed O'Ross is Itchy;

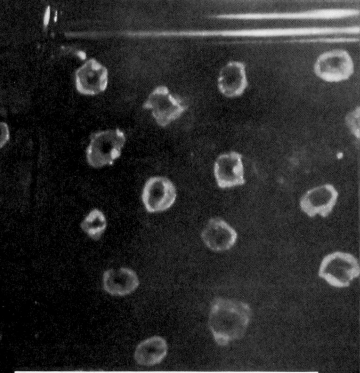

Flattop in the final shootout. When Chester Gould killed off Flattop in the comics, mournful fans sent flowers and staged a mock funeral outside the Chicago Tribune offices.

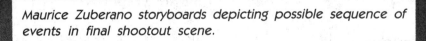

Maurice Zuberano storyboards depicting possible sequence of events in final shootout scene.

Paul Sorvino plays Lips Manlis; Henry Silva is Influence; and James Tolkin is Numbers.

The world of surprises in *Dick Tracy* includes cameo appearances by such familiar faces as John Schuck, Charles Fleisher (the voice of Roger Rabbit), Michael J. Pollard, Estelle Parsons, Allen Garfield, Mary Woronov, Henry Jones, and Kathy Bates.

With all the players and pieces in place, the production began principal photography at Universal Studios on February 2, 1989, and filmed for eighty-five days. The film was shot on 53 different interior sets, 25 exterior backlot sets and locations, and employed 305 cast, crew, and postproduction personnel. The post-production period lasted nearly a year. Beatty's company, Mulholland Productions, produced for Walt Disney Pictures.

In the end, it was what Warren Beatty had envisioned: an imaginary world that could reconcile beauty with disfigurement, violence with kindness, and good with evil. It was Dick Tracy on Film.

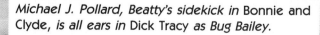

Michael J. Pollard, Beatty's sidekick in Bonnie and Clyde, *is all ears in* Dick Tracy *as Bug Bailey.*

A dirty deal leads Tracy to the Chinese Laundry, where the design of the scene is the stuff of comic strips. Simple geometric shapes, primary colors, and perfectly composed staging made each frame of the film a work of art.

Tracy chases the Kid, who has stolen a watch from a man at the diner.

WARREN BEATTY
and
"If I was going to arrest you, I'd have done it by now."
or
FAMOUS DETECTIVE GETS STAR TREATMENT

by CHESTER GOULD

"Warren Beatty," explained *Dick Tracy* production designer Richard Sylbert, who has done seven pictures with Beatty, "is a brain surgeon. *Your* brain. He asks more questions than any person I've ever met. The most-used word in his vocabulary is 'Why?'"

Ask people who work with him about Warren Beatty and you get a multiplicity of descriptions, but the theme that emerges most often is intelligence. The man is smart. Both sides of his family are educators. His father was a school superintendent, his grandmother the Dean of Women at Acadia University in Nova Scotia. As Sylbert put it, "He *inherited* something about smart." His restless intellect may be the reason he takes a long time to make his movies. He enjoys investigating every possibility before calling,

"Action!"

Beatty read the Dick Tracy comics as a kid, and wanted the film to recall a time of innocence in America.

Tracy narrowly escapes death following a drive-by shooting attempt by Flattop.

Like Dick Tracy interrogating Mumbles from behind the big lamp, Warren Beatty asks questions relentlessly, and you can't quite make him out behind the glare of that third-degree curiosity. Intelligence not only fuels his inherited need to know, it acts as his shield, his way of keeping the world at a comfortable distance, his yellow raincoat.

Who is Warren Beatty? It's a question that has intrigued movie audiences since he made his film debut in 1961 in *Splendor in the Grass,* directed by Elia Kazan. One answer might be that he's a man who enjoys having that question asked about him. Example: Composer Stephen Sondheim, who wrote Breathless Mahoney's songs for *Dick Tracy,* met Beatty for the first time at a party in New York. "He went straight to the piano and started to noodle," Sondheim recalled.

So he was soon the center of attention of the party, right?

"Quite the reverse," stressed the composer. *"Quite* the reverse. The piano was in another room entirely. Warren is not a partygoer, and it was his way of isolating himself. I heard the piano being played upstairs. I went upstairs and there he was." Who is Warren Beatty? If Hollywood is one big party, he's the music coming from the other room.

More than one of his collaborators likened him to Dick Tracy. A detective. A meticulous investigator. A man torn between family and duty, between light and shadow. Beatty himself said he was attracted to the movie because he "felt off the hook from the need to bring yet another dimension to the delineations between good and evil, love and temptation, love and duty, love and honor, personal obligations and societal obligations. They were all really there in that simple little comic strip. And the idea of doing a picture with a yellow hat and a yellow raincoat that matched seem like fun—if I could do it with the right people. So I did."

The script had been through many drafts, the most recent by Jim Cash and Jack Epps Jr., when Beatty agreed to play Dick Tracy. At first, he was only going to wear one hat, the yellow one. "It never occurred to me to direct the movie," he said. "But finally, like most of the movies that I direct, when the time comes to do it, I just do it because it's easier than going through what I'd have to go through to get somebody else to do it." (And redo it, he might have added.)

Once Beatty had signed on to direct and produce as well as star in the movie, he brought in Academy-

Award-winning writer Bo Goldman (*Melvin and Howard*) to rewrite the script. He also brought in Vittorio Storaro, his cinematographer on *Reds,* costume designer Milena Canonero, and Sylbert. And he started asking questions.

"He asks questions," reflected Sylbert, "because something tells him that everybody gets sloppy. Bureaucracies get set up." Added executive producer Barrie Osborne: "He pushes everything to the limit. He wants to know, in terms of story, that it's well thought out, that if somebody does something, it's smart. If Big Boy makes a move, he makes sure it's smart for Big Boy, not just because it lets Tracy win. It makes Tracy less of a hero if Big Boy is less clever. He thinks things through."

With the right group of people assembled, "you finally," Beatty observed, "get around to what you do." (And redo, he might have added. And debate.)

"He loves to get these different forces out on the table," said Osborne. "You've got very outspoken people on this film. He loves to get Dick Sylbert and Vittorio together, and they confront each other over

Tracy with sidekicks Pat Patton (James Keane, r.) and Sam Catchem (Seymour Cassel, l.).

Big Boy exhorts Breathless, as she and the girls of the Ritz Club rehearse "More."

Hard-boiled hero Tracy solves crime via what creator Chester Gould called "the hot lead route."

their different ideas, and out of that he gets a consensus. He has his own ideas, too, and he'll use that debate to test those ideas, to get what he wants."

Beatty continually asked his collaborators to defy the rules that they'd been taught and had lived by for most of their careers. "To make movies is generally to create a reality, to make it look real," he explained. "And this picture's sort of a style. The idea of having the primary colors match up, the idea of having things not look totally real, was hard for people to get. And everybody on the picture had difficulty with that. Because everybody's very good. There's no one better in the world than Vittorio, and so much of what he has been taught, and what he now teaches, is the reality of the situation, what he would call a photographic ideology. Reality was not our goal on this picture."

"Generally, a matte painter's craft is to make a painting look like reality. You couldn't go to a certain place, or get into a certain position, so you have a matte painting done that creates that look. Well, that's not exactly what we wanted here. We wanted it to look a little bit romantic, a little bit unreal, and that's a very tough job for a guy whose profession is matte painting."

How about a guy whose profession is acting? How did Beatty make Dick Tracy's character a little bit romantic, a little bit unreal? "I don't think it's smart to articulate

that," he reflected after a long pause. "I think it's dangerous to try and get too articulate about these things." Apparently when it comes to acting, intellect can be the enemy. Don't talk about it, just do it. When directing his fellow performers, Beatty often asked for so many takes that the actors were able to do the scene without thinking. Only then was the performance free enough to be a keeper. As Madonna described it: "His favorite thing to do is to do so many takes that you forget everything you planned on doing . . . and that's usually your best stuff."

His directing, like his acting, is instinctive, reactive. As Dick Tracy, he moves through the poisoned corruption of The City with the aplomb of a snake handler—knowing he won't get bitten, and knowing, too, that it's exciting for people to think maybe he will. The trademark Beatty eyes, wide-open, all-seeing, carry the audience along, so that Dick Tracy becomes not simply an object of their curiosity, but their ally in this adventure. And nothing he does as a director will get in the way.

"If you watch a picture directed by Warren Beatty," claimed production designer Sylbert, "I don't care which one . . . he is not fancy. He disappears, like I like to do. We've always said to each other, we don't like people who do 'Look at me, I'm here, too!'" He's got taste, certainly, but on the set you're looking at a man whose only interest is in the emotional dynamic of those characters."

Beatty put it another way: "I don't know what a style of directing is. It's hard to define, hard to articulate. You sit around with the script for a while, and then you try to make it happen. It's like when somebody asked Napoleon what his plan of battle was, he said, 'First we go there, and then we see what happens.'" Of course, he might have added, you go *prepared*.

The offspring of educators always did his homework. A perfect example was an acting class taught by the famed Stella Adler in the late 1950s in New York. Actor James Tolkin, who plays Numbers in *Dick Tracy*, was in the class with Beatty: "I'll never forget the first scene Warren did. It was a scene from *Our Town*, and here was this guy, he got up and played this scene, and when it was over and Warren had sat back down, Stella Adler got up in front of the class and she said like this, *'He's going to be a star!'* And she meant it. She said it with such fervor and of course Beatty believed it. And you know, when you believe, anything can happen."

Temptation. Breathless offers what Tess Trueheart cannot.

Anything can happen. It describes not only the arc of Warren Beatty's career, but a very appealing aspect of many of the roles he has chosen, including Dick Tracy. . . .

As Tracy, he sits in the opera with Tess, trying hard to appreciate the culture, trying hard to *learn* something, when he gets the call on his two-way wrist radio. He's got to go. When he goes, the movie audience goes with him, because we believe, as Warren Beatty believes, that *anything can happen.* The invitation to ride those canary-colored coattails proves irresistible.

Beatty's own personal journey toward the world of *Dick Tracy* began even before the Stella Adler class, when he was a boy back in Arlington, Virginia.

He set the film in the era of his childhood because it was "a period of my life that I like very much. There's something quaint about 1939, 1940 crime-fighting—the wrist radio, bugging a room with a huge microphone. I would just say that something about it moved me. I would say that prewar, just on the brink of war, there probably was a naïveté about America in that period, about good and evil, law and order. It's just before America took over. The last days of innocence. Just before our loss of innocence as a country."

He read the Chester Gould comics as research, but felt that they were limited in what the actors could learn from them. The two-dimensionality of the Gould characters left the performer's job undone. John Caglione and Doug Drexler, the makeup artists, fleshed out the appearances of the villains, but Beatty decided that "the major feeling characters, the ones with whom we empathize the most" would go without prosthetics. He thought that "to make one constantly aware of these makeups, as the screen will do, would've been a distraction to what was important.

"I went through all the prosthetic things. But nobody's going to look like (the comic book) Dick Tracy and occupy the audience in the way the character needs to in this movie. It's very hard to put those grotesque makeups onto Dick Tracy or Tess Trueheart or the Kid— it is just too distracting. The makeup runs away with it. In the characters of Flattop, Pruneface, Big Boy—that's something else. That's where it works."

One of the actors who made it work was Al Pacino as Big Boy. Pacino played with the prosthetics until they stirred a character in him that became Big Boy Caprice, nutcracker *par excellence.* Pacino's portrayal never failed, in turn, to stir Beatty. "I never worked with a more interesting actor than Al. I could be depressed and almost asleep, and Al comes on the set and starts doing things, and he just really amuses me. He's funny. He has intensity, he has intelligence, he has energy, he has everything. What I wanted to do with the guy was to—" Beatty stopped. "You see, I don't believe in talking about these things," he said, almost apologetically. The Director had nearly stepped on the Actor. One gets the distinct idea that Writing, Directing, and Producing are a series of protective cocoons he builds around his productions to safeguard the Acting, to ensure that his cast has the best possible environment in which to nurture the delicate balance of emotions that become the story.

"I presume it must be a somewhat schizophrenic experience for him," said editor Richard Marks, of the

Tracy talks into his wrist radio—another of the simple gimmicks that harkened Beatty back to a more innocent era.

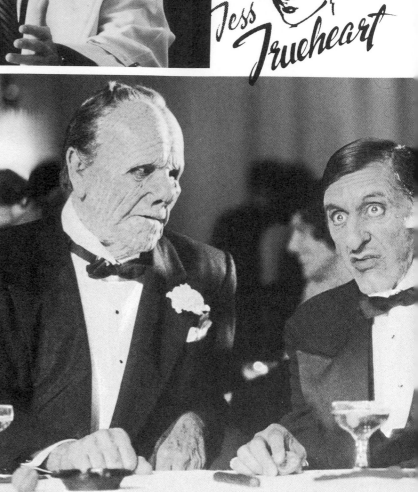

Tracy and Tess Trueheart. Their relationship forms the emotional bedrock of the story.

Intensity radiates from every pore of Tracy's face. Driven but controlled, the detective must meet the challenges presented by his love life, his enemies, and the Kid.

multiple-credit demands of Beatty's job. "I find it funny sometimes when we're sitting and looking over a cut and I'll be talking to him and I won't know whether to say 'Dick Tracy' or *'you.'* My mind kind of reels. Who am I talking to? Usually, Marks explained, he refers to a character in a film by the character's name, "but if you're talking to the person who *is* Dick Tracy, you don't know what to say. It's like you're stuck for a pronoun."

Bonnie and Clyde was the first of six films Beatty had produced. It served notice to the Hollywood community that he had the foresight to nurture a film from the scripted page to the Oscar ceremonies. He has since been nominated for eleven Academy Awards (Best Actor and Best Picture, *Bonnie and Clyde;* Best Screenplay, *Shampoo;* Actor, Picture, Screenplay, Director for *Heaven Can Wait;* Actor, Picture, Screenplay, Director for *Reds*), and won the Oscar for directing *Reds.* The man asks questions, and the man gets some pretty satisfactory answers.

Of Beatty's skills as a producer, his longtime friend Sylbert said, "He's a great negotiator, loves it. He does all the producing. He doesn't delegate anything to anybody. And I must tell you that Warren's ability to say

'Why?' drove Vittorio crazy at the beginning of this picture. He said to me, 'I just spent two years thinking about this movie, why do I have to negotiate every idea I have with Warren?' Warren said, 'That's me, Vittorio. That's who I am. If I'm not that, I'm nothing.' You don't sell him an idea," said Sylbert, "you have to prove it."

"You may think you've come to a conclusion, resolved something," concluded executive producer Osborne. "At a certain point in time, Warren is likely to reopen the question." It is Beatty's way of getting the best out of people, making them reexamine their positions, getting them to *do their homework*. "He does it himself," Osborne noted. "He agonizes over whether the story is right, whether he's taking the easy way out, or really thinking it through."

That Warren Beatty can be so agonizingly absorbed with the writing, directing, and producing of a movie—and set aside those thoughts when the camera rolls, so that he can *just act*—must surely be genius, or something akin to it. Whatever you choose to call this gift, it is the reason that we believe *Dick Tracy*'s world, it is the reason we can set aside our own thoughts at the theater door, settle in as he gets that first call on the wrist radio, and *just watch*.

Nemesis. Al Pacino's portrayal of Big Boy Caprice "never failed to amuse" the director and enlivened the entire production.

Video-assist monitors let the director observe the star after a take. Beatty, according to production manager Jon Landau, used the video primarily to assess the framing of a shot, not to judge the actors' performances.

Madonna changed her hair from long and brunette to short and blond for Dick Tracy because Vittorio Storaro liked the light in her golden locks.

Madonna strikes a pose worthy of Dietrich.

MADONNA
and
"Does it seem hot to you?"
or
MOB THRUSH TIED TO CAPRICE

"Madonna." The name conjures up enough adjectives to exhaust a dictionary. Sexy, sultry, sensational, seductive, seismic, sensual, shapely—and these are only the *S*'s.

Madonna. It may be the most marquee-ready name in the entertainment business, but it didn't come ready-made. Madonna Ciccone refined her image from the raw material of a large, midwestern Italian Catholic family, burnished it performing in the fiery trials of New York's rock scene, and publicized it with her huge successes in the music business.

Not your basic "shake an' bake" pop star, but a talented young woman who sensed that her roots could support her stratospheric growth as a performer, Madonna branched out: To the film business with the title role in *Desperately Seeking Susan*. To the bright lights of Broadway in David Mamet's *Speed-the-Plow*. She mixes her media without missing a beat.

To the question asked by marquee watchers the world over—What's next?—only Madonna knows the answer. What's now? She answered that one with her sexy-sultry-sensational-seductive-seismic-sensual-shapely performance as Breathless Mahoney in *Dick Tracy*.

Breathless comes on to Dick Tracy with all the subtlety of a steam locomotive. She wields her sex like a weapon, daring the buttoned-down detective to duel on her terms, hoping to make him a hostage of her love and spring her from life as a mob moll. Her siren song, in turn, tests Tracy as a hero. He must lash himself to the mast of righteousness and sail on.

Madonna's pose-crazy portrayal of Breathless ties knots in the classic lines of the love story. All her skills as a performer come into play. The Material Girl vamps it up in "More," a song about never having enough; professes her true-blue love for Tracy in a duet with Mandy Patinkin, "What Can You Lose?"; and acts like Anything But A Virgin in the rest of the film. Her background as a dancer certainly helped her essay a character whose brain is a sophomore but whose body is a Ph.D.

In her interview for this book, Madonna proved as down-to-earth as a multinational megastar could possibly be. Big Italian families have a way of keeping even a megastar's feet on the ground. She was funny, she was pleasant, she was patient. Her remarks follow, in their semientirety.

Q: Tell us about Breathless, her history. Where did she come from?

MADONNA: (laughs, yawns) She's in a pretty bad situation to begin with. I mean anybody who accepts the life that she was leading obviously comes from a ****** place. She's got a job singing in a nightclub, she's not a successful singer. I mean I don't think she's making records and stuff, or she wouldn't be there. And she stays there and takes the abuse of whatever gangster takes over, bullies his way into the club. She has this tough exterior, but there are many moments of vulnerability throughout the movie where you see who she really is—a person with a lot of pain who's never really been loved, and she wants to get out of it. And that's what she sees when she sees Dick Tracy. Because Dick Tracy treats her with respect for the first time. No other man has, so that's why she falls madly in love with him.

Q: He's the sun and you're the moon.
MADONNA: Exactly. *El sol y la luna.*

Q: What did the role of Breathless have that you like in a movie part?
MADONNA: I wanted to work with Warren and all the other actors who were doing it. I thought the script

"She's just a big poser," Madonna said of her character in the film. Here, Breathless assumes a classic torch-singer pose.

Breathless Mahoney as she appeared in the Dick Tracy comic strip in the '30s . . .

. . . and updated to the '90s.

was very funny. Style's a big thing for me, and I just thought it was going to be a really original piece of work. Something different.

Q: What were you shown of the film's design before taking the role?

MADONNA: All I saw were drawings of the characters. I read some comic strips. I read the script. I kind of got an idea what it was going to look like from Warren and Vittorio Storaro, and Milena. Breathless is larger than life. She has the most incredible costumes. She doesn't go anywhere unless she's wearing an evening gown. It's totally outrageous and insane, and it's fun to be able to play somebody like that. The challenge of it is to take it one step beyond the cartoon character, which is so one-dimensional, and to add to it.

Q: How did you humanize the comic-strip Breathless?

MADONNA: By dealing with the basic issues in her life, and that is that this is a girl who's trapped. By thinking of her in a human way, even though she is all glitter and gold and platinum-blond hair.

Q: What kind of input did you have into the way Breathless looked?

MADONNA: It didn't come easily. It was trial and error. I felt like a mannequin on wheels for a while, because, first of all, I had finally grown my hair out, and it was long and dark, and they couldn't decide if they should make Breathless blond or brunette. So I did a screen test in a blond wig and of course Vittorio Storaro started ooohing and aaahing, so that was really it. Something about the light around your face when your hair is blond, and the backlighting. So my long hair kept getting chopped off, more and more and more . . . it was a hair-raising experience. Breathless couldn't have one of those beautiful Lana Turner hairdos, because Lana Turner was too pulled together. I spent more time figuring out Breathless's character in terms of the way she looked than anything else—trying on the dresses, deciding how far we were going to go with her . . . undressing, and the way her hair was going to look. The thing we were trying to capture with Breathless is that when we see her she always just got dragged out of bed.

Q: Who were your inspirations for the character?

MADONNA: The only person that I could even think of in terms of an inspiration—and she's not even right because she's too hard and masculine, she was just invulnerable—was Marlene Dietrich. You know that stance she always had when she performed where she was just not going to give you too much? She dared you to like her, in a way. She wouldn't make a move toward you, she wouldn't kiss an audience's ***, you know? In terms of performing, I thought of her. I wish I could've looked more like her, but that's Marlene Dietrich, you know? A girl like that wouldn't have been stuck in a situation like Breathless.

Q: Tell us about the Stephen Sondheim songs you sang for the film. How were they presented to you?

MADONNA: Stephen Sondheim played the songs on the piano for me one day in Warren's living room. He sang them to me in his most-endearing fashion. I thought, "Omigod, I have to sing *those songs?*"

Q: Why did you react like that?

MADONNA: Because they're very complex songs. They're not like any songs I've ever sung, and they're not even like obvious pop songs from that era. The chordal and rhythmic changes made them complicated. That's the way Stephen writes, he never repeats himself, wordwise or notewise. And he just doesn't give in, he doesn't resolve things musically. You know when you hear a song and you know what's coming next? He doesn't do that. So they're very difficult to learn. And when I heard them, I didn't want to like them, I resisted them, except for "I'll Always Get My Man," which I liked.

Q: How did you go about learning them?

MADONNA: I decided that I was going to think of it as a challenge, it was going to be like learning how to tap dance, which was very complex, and which I had to do for *Bloodhounds of Broadway.* I got a voice coach, Seth Riggs, and he helped me find the notes, because going from one note to the next was so strange. Seth's accompanist would make slowed-down versions of the songs and I would take them home and memorize them, just go over and over them. And then we started having rehearsals with (choreographer) Jeffrey Hornaday for the staging of them, and that's what really brought them to life for me. Not to be standing in my kitchen singing them. They were just songs to me before I got into a performance situation and put on a long dress to rehearse in. When I present them, that's when they come to life for me.

Q: You strike a lot of strong poses in the film, for instance, appearing in Dick Tracy's doorway with a bottle of champagne . . .

MADONNA: That's Breathless Mahoney. She's just a big poser.

Q: Did you have a favorite pose in the picture, one that really captured the character?

MADONNA: One of the first times you see me in the movie, Dick Tracy comes back to the dressing room to see me, and I'm changing behind one of those screens, and I put on a negligee and come out . . . and I strike this pose knowing he can see through my negligee, holding the champagne glass in the air. It was ridiculous. (laughs) Nobody acts that way. And I'm doing it just right, so that I'm silhouetted on the wall behind me. Actually, Marlene Dietrich used to do that all the time, too. I mean the girl was more interested in hitting her mark than anything. All she ever did was pose. She knew where the light was. And that's what Breathless did, too. She was so much about light. So . . . her life may be miserable, but she always looks good.

Q: When Breathless visits Tracy in his office, she says, "There's a pool of darkness in you, Tracy. And I'm here to take a swim." Does that sum up their relationship?

MADONNA: I always felt so ridiculous saying those lines, so we'd do it as written, and then we'd try something that was a little bit less over the top. But what she means is that—Dick Tracy walks around trying to be like a cheerleader. He's so good and you can't tap it, you can't break that veneer of Mr. All-American Hero. So Breathless is saying she knows there's something else going on behind there—which is true, I mean the guy's psychotic. He avoids intimacy with people and he's addicted to catching bad guys. There's something crazy about his behavior—a guy who goes around talking to his wrist watch. She knows he has a dark side, and she calls him on it. "I know you're interested in me, so why don't you stop pretending that you're not?"

Q: In your view, are Breathless Mahoney and Tess Trueheart two halves of a whole woman?

MADONNA: I never thought of it that way. I always thought that Tess Trueheart was a bitch, I hated her guts.

Q: Why?

MADONNA: Because she gets Dick Tracy. She's got dibs on him, let's just say that. She has his passion. She has his loyalty. I guess you could do the obvious, and think that she was this kind of wimpy girl, this goody-two-shoes kind of person. A saint. But I think Glenne Headly portrayed her with strength, a sense of humor, and vulnerability. And you could do the same with Breathless and say that she was just the bad girl, and only the bad girl. I don't think I played her that way. The only thing Tess and Breathless had that was similar was equal amounts of self-contempt. Tess hated the fact that she couldn't look good in a backless evening gown . . . and Breathless can look at Tess and hate the fact that she can never have Dick Tracy's love.

Q: Describe working with Warren Beatty.

MADONNA: Hmmm . . . (laughs) . . . hmmm. Warren is an interesting man. This is the time when I wish I had control over really big multisyllabic words. Warren is . . . well, he's kind of like Dick Tracy.

Q: How so?

MADONNA: Dick Tracy is a very isolated guy, as far as I'm concerned. He's kind of a loner. He's also very smart, very clever. He's also a detective. And Warren is all of those things. He investigates everything, from the shoes on your feet to the bow in your hair. Nothing goes by him. He studies people intensely and he has this way of extracting information out of you, and you realize after you've spilled all the beans that you've just told this perfect stranger everything, and he hasn't told you anything. Everybody does that with him. He does something to you that makes you, obviously, comfortable to do that. It's not a cold investigation—he seduces you into telling him things. So I guess I would have to say he's seductive.

Q: Describe his directing method.

MADONNA: He's a perfectionist. You can't get away with anything with him. In terms of acting, he's relentless, and if it takes a hundred takes to get it, then you're going to do a hundred takes. He's very generous, in that you can try whatever you want with him. But his favorite thing to do is to do so many takes that you forget everything you planned on doing, and you're completely broken down, and then you just do it without thinking, and that's usually your best stuff.

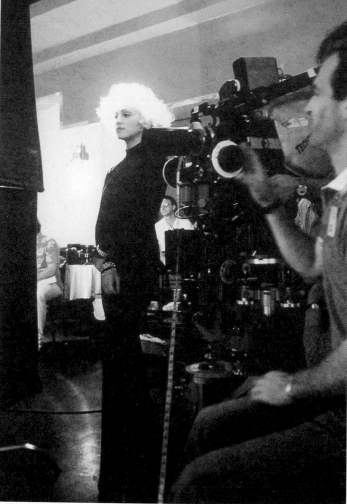

Mandy Patinkin, as 88 Keys, sings of his love for Breathless, but she's singing about Dick Tracy, in "What Can You Lose," written by Stephen Sondheim.

Hair ablaze with light, Madonna waits off-camera for her cue.

"He treated me like a bad little girl . . . I thought he was a gross pig," said Madonna of Breathless's relationship with Big Boy.

Warren Beatty rehearses a scene featuring Madonna and the Club Ritz dancers. "His favorite thing," she reported, "was to ask for so many takes you forgot what you had planned to do . . . that was usually the best stuff."

Q: What was the most difficult scene for you?

MADONNA: The waterfront. Because I wanted to let go of everything at that point and let him see how desperate I really was. I saw it as a woman who didn't care anymore, who didn't care about keeping up the hard façade and the posing. Warren wanted me to play it invulnerable, as well. He wanted to do it both ways. So we did the scene take after take where I was devastated, falling apart, until I thought I was done. I went back to my trailer and he let me calm down, and then a half an hour later he came to the trailer and said that he wanted me to come out and do it all over again. I said *"What?"* And I had to go out and play it all over again as invulnerable.

Q: Describe the relationship between Breathless and Big Boy.

MADONNA: I had nothing but contempt for Big Boy. And he would treat me like a bad little girl. He was always slapping me and spanking me. And in terms of being on the set, whenever Al put his prosthetics on, his suit, he was a gross pig. And he's not that way in real life—he's very gracious, and well-mannered, and gentlemanly, and sweet. . . . As Big Boy, he would tell me the dirtiest jokes and suck on his cigar like it was some sort of weird phallic symbol, and just be a pig. He was always smacking my butt and my face. I hated him, I loathed him, I was disgusted with him. And so what happened off-camera was that I'd always try to be moving away from him, and he'd always grab me and go "Get over here!" which is exactly what happened in

the movie. Every time I expressed my distaste for him, he would smack me, which is also what happened in the movie. I got mad. He made me cry sometimes. There was a scene where he kept smacking me in the stomach, and it would sting, and what made me cry was not so much the hit, but the fact that Warren wouldn't stop. He would just keep going, and I was humiliated. So it worked, because that's what's happening to Breathless—she's totally humiliated by Big Boy.

Q: Did you always stay in character off-camera?

MADONNA: Yes. I always do, in all my movies.

Q: There must be some similarities, then, between you and Breathless. . . .

MADONNA: Yeah, we both like Warren. (laughs) Other than that, she's a victim, I'm not. She's a singer, I am. She's sexy, I am. I don't think that people are only going to like me if I go around looking fabulous and posing all the time, and that's what Breathless thinks. So there are some similarities, and there aren't. But I think people are attracted to doing characters that have something to do with themselves, that they can relate to deep down inside.

Q: What will be happening to Breathless after this movie?

MADONNA: She's going to go to the hospital. She'll be in and out of rehabs. As for the rest, it'll have to be a mystery.

Breathless Mahoney's desperation reveals a heart of darkness in Dick Tracy.

VISUAL EFFECTS
and
" . . . . I have a vision.
A Big Boss must always
have a vision."
Or
CITY "AN ILLUSION"
CLAIM WITNESSES

Michael Lloyd and Harrison Ellenshaw had, between them, been all over the universe: From the Ice Planet in *The Empire Strikes Back* to the farmlands of Iowa in *Country*, and various intergalactic locations along the way. As two of the premier visual effects artists in the film business, their job had always been to make a picture look real. To make the audience believe in the chilling vastness of the planet Hoth, or in the tornado that swept down on Jessica Lange's harvest-setting.

On *Dick Tracy*, their job was to make the picture look "unreal." To lead the audience into a great, big, audaciously colored comic strip on film.

Primarily through the use of fifty-seven matte shots combining live-action with painted backgrounds, Ellenshaw and Lloyd anchored *Dick Tracy* in a world that set all the old precepts about matte painting askew, a world somewhere between Reality and Toon Town. "Superreal," Warren Beatty described the look he

The drawbridge model ready for shooting. The drawbridge and train were built and photographed by Stetson Visuals of Los Angeles.

A miniature sightseeing boat passes under the drawbridge, heightening the excitement of the final confrontation between the main characters.

A camera's-eye view of the drawbridge raising to let the sightseeing boat pass.

wanted. "A half a turn of the screw" was makeup man John Caglione's phrase. The visual effects people had their name for the movie's mythical setting: "Tracy Town."

The generic City of *Dick Tracy* was originally designed by Richard Sylbert's art department, which outlined it in bold strokes of comic-book colors. Director of photography Vittorio Storaro painted the sets in fiercely contrasting light and shadow. The Buena Vista artists took it to the sky.

"In some scenes, we had ninety-eight percent of the frame to make up," said Michael Lloyd, whose Buena Vista Visual Effects Group oversees effects for most Disney and Touchstone films. Lloyd designed the "opening of the ark" scene in *Raiders of the Lost Ark,* as well as effects for such films as *Splash* and *Outrageous Fortune.* Yet his work had never been so squarely in the spotlight as on *Dick Tracy.* "It's like a painting that you'd do as an artist. You compose the shot, add color and density—trying to make the image stand on its own."

The film opens at sunset and ends at sunrise, days later. The opening scene, with the Kid dodging down the alley next to the Seventh Street Garage, featured the film's first matte painting, catalogued by the productions as "M-1." With the City silhouetted in the final

A painted flat straddling the railroad tracks . . .

Production designer Sylbert peers through the lens as Storaro (l.) and Michael Lloyd look on.

fireburst of daylight, "M-1" struck a dramatic opening note. Said Harrison Ellenshaw: "The reason it was decided to make the first scene in the movie a matte shot was to get us immediately into *Tracy*'s environment—so M-1 was the most important matte in a way. Because it took the whole issue of exactly where we were off the audience's mind. There was a ton of exposition in that one matte. We're in a comic book. Boom. You're into the characters and the story, and it all meshes perfectly with that first thirty-second shot."

Ellenshaw had done effects on some big projects in his career—*Star Wars, The Empire Strikes Back, Tron, Captain Eo*—and matte paintings had never been so vital in establishing the look of a picture. "Usually, you give the audiences as much reality as you can, then sneak a matte shot in there and hope nobody notices it. In this movie the matte paintings *are* the reality."

Dick Tracy utilized nearly every technique in the arsenal of Buena Vista Visual Effects. In addition to the fifty-seven matte paintings, they produced a miniature smoke-belching train and trainyard, a miniature drawbridge with its own river and ferryboat, ten blue-screen traveling matte shots, and one scene using a process exclusive to the Disney Studios, the Sodium Screen traveling matte process.

Visual effects, in the parlance of Hollywood film production, are not the same as special effects. Special effects take place on the set—with crashing cars, explosions, gunshots, breaking glass, and gushing water. Visual effects, on the other hand, come alive in the quiet of postproduction, with film stock, computers, paintings, masking tape, miniatures, cameras, and optical printers. Special effects people are into physics and like to play outdoors. Visual effects artists tend to be indoor types, chemists in their laboratories of light.

Glenn Campbell, a visual effects cameraman on *Dick Tracy,* wrote rhapsodically of the illusions achieved by his outdoor counterparts in live-action special effects: "During the . . . battle between Big Boy's henchmen and the cops, some of the guns are not real guns firing blanks, but are modified guns hooked up to off-screen acetelyne gas tanks, which produce long-duration bursts of flame that photograph better for motion pictures.

"The bullet-hits that spell out D-I-C-K T-R-A-C-Y, the ferocious steam hissing out of the deadly boiler, the gouts of flame that leap out of the overturned cars, these are the works of the special effects man."

When a scene gets too risky for performers or too big for a budget, the *visual effects* artists take over in the relative safety and economy of postproduction. The

. . . combined with Tracy and his yellow attire complete the tableau.

Richard Sylbert's conceptual design for Tracy and Breathless's tryst at the waterfront.

The visual effects artists painted a cityscape to loom over Tess' greenhouse, which was shot as a live action plate on the backlot at Universal Studios.

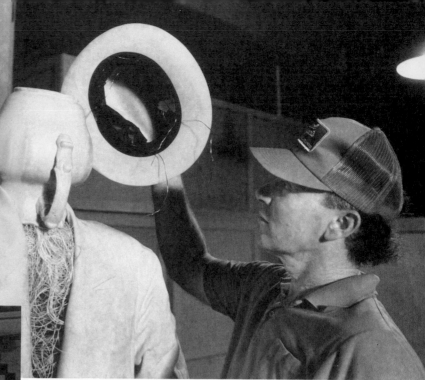

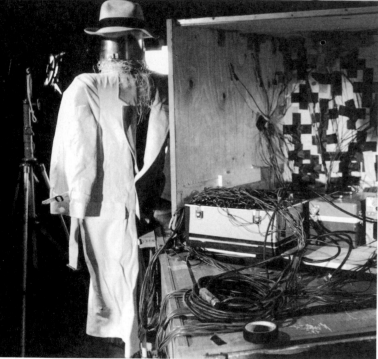

The Dick Tracy decoy was wired with squibs, which detonated when submachine bullets "hit" it. An example of a special, as opposed to visual, effect.

A rough composite of what the finished waterfront scene would look like.

Buena Vista Visual Effects group is the heir to a storied tradition of Disney film effects. From *Treasure Island* through *Mary Poppins* and *Honey, I Shrunk the Kids,* Disney's visual effects had always helped define the style of the movie they were in. And that's what Beatty and company wanted on *Dick Tracy.* Vittorio Storaro, in particular, was moved by the color of the night skies in *A Hundred and One Dalmatians.*

The buildings on Universal Studios' backlot are three stories tall, the longest street is four blocks. The movie would suffocate if confined to those exterior dimensions. Job Number One at Buena Vista Effects was giving *Dick Tracy* room to breathe. "Our department enabled the movie to open up in scope by using matte paintings, which not only made Universal's buildings

taller by adding extra floors, but also created the entire City around them," explained Lloyd.

The City. Tracy Town. It would become the single most-debated concept in the production of *Dick Tracy,* because, as the visual capper on the look of the film, it was the last say anybody would have. And besides, critiques of matte paintings usually center on whether

*Live-action of the scene in front of the
department store without the matte painting.*

or not they look like the real thing. *Dick Tracy* production meetings had an odd existential twist: The question was not whether a painting looked like a skyline, but whether it look like a *Dick Tracy* skyline. And then the question was, *what* is a *Dick Tracy* skyline? It seemed, at times, to lead them in maddening circles in search of their mythical City.

With matte artists Michelle Moen, Paul Lasaine, Lucy Tanashian, and Tom Gilleon, the Buena Vista Group enlarged the colors of the sets and costumes into a City that aroused the fantasy of setting foot inside a comic strip. One way in which they captured the comic-strip mood was the atmosphere—there was none. "In each and every shot we've got a crystal-clear sky. Intense color going from a cyan to a deep purple," said Lloyd. "I think the key to it is the colorization of the sky and buildings." "We can pretty much play any games we want with color," added matte artist Lasaine.

The games they played with color were designed to retain the comic-book qualities of the design ethic, while not letting the film cross the line from Tracy Town into Toon Town. Paul Lasaine elaborated on their tightrope act: "We could follow the color scheme and have every ten-year-old in the audience scream 'Look at the matte!' or we could generate realistic paintings and dilute the comic style of the live-action." The final paintings carefully balanced the two styles.

While *Dick Tracy* pushed the possibilities of mattes to a new extreme, the art of matte painting is nearly as old as the motion picture business itself. Cameraman Glenn Campbell described how a matte shot is created:

"A matte painting can be created by several different methods, all of which require photography of the actors first, creating what is known as the 'live-action plate.' Once the live-action has been shot, it is projected onto a sheet of white spray-painted glass. The live-action is traced by an artist onto the glass, clearly marking portions where the actors are positioned. The artist will also trace all architectural highlights and perspectives. Using a print of the live-action plate as a guide, the artist will match the color of every building in the tracing and extend the tracing upwards to now include new buildings and perhaps a sky. At this point, the portion that contained the original live-action is scraped away, leaving a clear window of glass at the bottom of the new painting. Now the effects cameraman places a sheet of translucent plastic on the back of the window, which permits him to project the live-action footage from behind the glass onto what is, in effect, a miniature movie screen. Viewed from the front

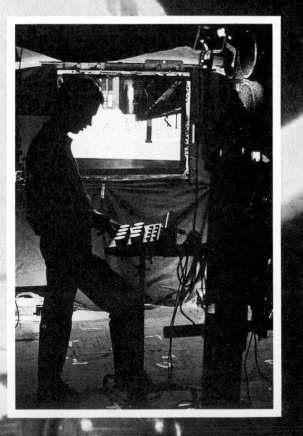

A computer-controlled camera composites the matte painting of the elevated train tracks with live-action on separate passes of the film through the camera.

side, the cameraman can photograph both the live action and the painting, using whatever filters and exposures are necessary to combine both images on film."

Combining images on film defines the work of the visual effects artist. The scene in which the Kid escapes Tracy by ducking in front of the train links live-action, a matte painting, and a miniature train.

Tracy and the Kid were filmed as they ran down one hundred feet of fake train track laid out on the Universal backlot, playing out their chase against an empty set. Six months later, there would be a roaring steam locomotive joining them in the shot.

Master modelmaker Mark Stetson and his company, Stetson Visual Services, were brought in to supervise

Visual effects supervisor Michael Lloyd airbrushed an illustration that would serve as the model for the matte painting.

A miniature steam locomotive combines with live-action and matte painting to create the scene in the trainyard.

the construction of a 150-foot by 35-foot trainyard, complete with a miniature steam train supplied by a private collector. Veteran model photographer Bill Neil and camera assistant Peter Montgomery spent weeks getting the shot to work.

"It was a real steam-powered train," explained Montgomery, "but we needed a computer-controlled train so that we could shoot various film elements for combination later in the optical department. We needed to be able to create a train element, a matte element, and a steam element, which meant the train had to have repeatable movement, which can only be achieved by motion control. So we converted the steam engine to puff smoke, but not power the wheels. That was left up to our computer." (Motion control is the motion-

Big Boy tows Tess Trueheart in front of a blue screen, which permits the addition of a complete background matte.

A room in the matte department at Buena Vista Visual Effects, located on the Disney Studios lot. Beatty and the production team selected Buena Vista for visual effects work because of its tradition of using mattes to create imaginary settings.

picture application of computers to model photography. A computer controls a series of motors attached to a motion-picture camera, enabling the operator to repeat a camera movement as many times as needed. The cameraman can thus execute complicated camera moves and modify them or even call them back up months later from the computer's memory.)

"We connected a long cable to the train," continued Montgomery, "and dragged it with a powerful servomotor we'd hooked into the computer. Mind you, we were dragging a metal train that was two feet tall and forty feet long, and its total weight was literally one ton. Our problems occurred as soon as we tried to slow down the train after the shot had been completed. You can't overcome that much mass and inertia easily. The train would have plowed into the camera during our head-on shot. We wound up placing a surfaced mirror on the tracks and shooting the reflection of the train as it raced toward us. At the last minute, Fred Albrecht, our key grip, would flip the mirror out of the way so it wouldn't get smashed. It was tricky, but it worked."

Because of the different lighting requirements for each, the smoke was photographed separately from the train itself. The train was exposed at one frame per second, the smoke at sixty frames per second. These two elements were then combined on an optical printer with the matte painting and the live-action plate to complete the scene.

Stetson Visual Services also created a beautifully detailed miniature drawbridge and ferryboat packed with passengers for the film's climactic sequence. However, it was what they did with the "water" that made the miniature pay off.

As Glenn Campbell writes: "Water and fire have always been the bane of effects men who strive to film realistic miniature settings. Although bricks, trees, even people, can be constructed convincingly, a match flame or a drop of water always looks the same size. Enlarging a tiny flame does not make it appear to be a roaring inferno, and one ripple in a pool never looks like a wave, no matter how much it's magnified."

Taking the limits of miniaturization into account, Stetson and crew cut out a large strip of rippled Plexiglas, not unlike a bumpy shower door. Placed under the miniature lights of the bridge, the reflections on the Plexiglas created a convincing impression of rippling river water.

The elements of the drawbridge miniatures were designed to work in combination with a matte painting, and sometimes also a live-action plate, such as Big Boy's car approaching the dockside warehouse. These elements were composited on the matte camera.

Actors and miniatures were combined optically using a traveling matte. As Al Pacino dragged Glenne Headly up the rising drawbridge, he did so in front of a special blue screen designed to generate a matte. The optical department could then isolate an image of the actors, which was combined later with the background plate of the drawbridge model to create the finished scene.

For the opera scene, Disney's fabled Sodium Screen process permitted the filmmakers to combine a close-up shot of Tracy and Tess with the singers in the background and the extras in the audience—all in impossibly sharp focus. This technique, which also creates a traveling matte, uses sodium-vapor lamps to light up a yellow screen while photographing the live-action with a custom-made camera. Unlike blue-screen mattes, Sodium Screen allows any color in the costumes and any color lighting, which is why Tracy and Tess can enjoy the bright blue opera while Tracy wears his trademark yellow raincoat.

Dick Tracy rewards an audience simply because it puts the best work of a talented group of people on display. It took two people like Michael Lloyd and Harrison Ellenshaw, whose imaginations have taken them everywhere, to come up with a place the movies hadn't been to before—Tracy Town.

They had a lot of help, of course. Matte photography was by David Hardberger, Richard Kendall, Steven Brooks, and Glenn Campbell. Optical photography was by Kevin Koneval and Douglas Ulm, under the supervision of Steven Rundell. Jim Mann handled the original color negative. Gernie Gagliano and Robert Yamamoto oversaw the optical line-up and effects editing, respectively. Animator Allan Gonzales enhanced many of the mattes with his artwork. Lynda Lemon, Brooke Benton, Carolyn Soper, and Melissa Taylor managed and coordinated the production. The departmental production was overseen by Jacobus Rose.

Beatty checks the framing as Storaro checks the sunlight. The director, said Storaro, saw the scene from the point of view of the character.

PHOTOGRAPHY
and
"You tried the iodine transfer and the silver nitrate?"
or
STORARO "BEST IN WORLD" SAYS BEATTY

Vittorio Storaro was inspired.

"The original comic strip was our bible," observed the director of photography, whose dazzling camera work rocketed *Dick Tracy* into a new dimension of cinema art. Studying those long-ago Sunday funnies, Storaro was struck by Chester Gould's hard-hitting use of color. "What really touched me," recalled Storaro in his Italian-flavored English, "was using primary color to tell the characters. One of the most important recognitions of Dick Tracy is the yellow raincoat and yellow hat."

Yellow? *Important?* What Storaro had done was

pick Dick Tracy's pocket, dipping into that yellow raincoat for the key to a bold cinematic color scheme. This is where Storaro shines. Painting the precise colors of dramatic conflict has been a career obsession. "When I faced Dick Tracy, I was trying to investigate the symbolism, the physiology, the *meaning* of each color." Yellow became the first spoke of a spinning color wheel that set off a shower of creative sparks.

"Given a specific connection between one color and one character," the movie revealed itself to Storaro as "a dramatic fight between warm color and cold color. Between light and shadow. YELLOW represents the color of the sun. This is Dick Tracy." When Tracy's sun set, the BLUE moon of Big Boy Caprice rose. The evil evening spawned "powers drawing their color from oppression, from crime, from bullying."

Gradually, other characters were keyed into the picture. On the sunny side of the street, the Kid watched it all happen with an emotional blush of RED. Mix his rosy color with Tracy's yellow and you find yourself basking in the warm ORANGE of Tess Trueheart.

District Attorney Fletcher was "in the GREEN oscillation between yellow and blue, between good and evil. He superimposed the one on the other without joining the two opposing elements." Flattop, Pruneface, and Mumbles are INDIGO-keyed grotesques who only come out at night.

According to Storaro, VIOLET-hued Breathless was "a creature lighted by the color of blood and the light of the moon." She completes the magic color-wheel in which the elements are counterposed. Practically the entire cast of the movie has been represented in the color spectrum.

"Each color carries one specific vibration on our hearts, on our eyes. It changes our attitude when we face that specific color. We were trying to use color to dramatize the story, to emphasize the characters.

"These are not the kind of colors the audience is used to seeing," noted Storaro. "These are much more dramatic in strength, in saturation." Besides, "it's not only the palette of the color, it's the usage of the color." Storaro's colors splash off the characters and soak into their surroundings. For instance, everything yellow—including a taxicab—is made to look the same canary shade as Dick Tracy's hat and raincoat. When Big Boy blusters into a scene, all the blues take their cues from him. Identical colors bounce off each other like reflections in a funhouse mirror.

Still, Storaro was not satisfied. "It is not enough," he admitted, "to use only primary colors." Lurking in the shadows, looming over all of *Dick Tracy,* is the brooding absence of color itself. "BLACK to me, especially in this movie, is like a major character. Because when Dick Tracy is fighting against the black of night, it represents a very dramatic element." Black, of course, is the escutcheon of the mysterious stranger know only as The Blank. To Storaro, black resonates "an absorption of all colors, whether good or evil. Black is the dark container into which Blank places the whole of his unbridled will for power."

Storaro insisted on "the dramatic look of a very

In this shot, the yellow color of justice explodes onto the night.

Tracy brought the color of sunlight with him wherever he went.

The cold blue light of evil gave scenes such as this one a nightmarish quality.

Breathless's bobtail speedster roars onto an indigo street with pink puddles.

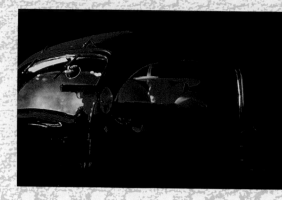

The Blank—a character who is "not light, but darkness made visible." Black, the absence of color, became a major character in Storaro's scheme of things.

A study in scarlet—Tracy in a two-color composition by Storaro.

strong black. *Dick Tracy* has to represent two different areas in impossible embrace, day and night, light and shadow; and color and black-and-white. To cement that impossible embrace, Storaro relied on the ENR film process, which links a separate black-and-white negative to the color negative to create the finished positive image of the picture.

"It makes the original combination of colors, plus the black, much better, much more dramatic. It makes the black very, very strong, very, very important." ENR's sinewy, seductive shade of black supercharges the visual conflict. "It changes a little bit the separation of the color itself. That is the originality of this picture. Normally, colors have been used for comedy, or something light. Here we are trying to use color for something very dramatic, and, too, very specific."

Storaro's cinematography is a symphony of contrasting hues, a counterpoint of light and darkness, a rhythmic variation of silhouettes and polished portraits. "From a graphic point of view, I was trying to be very, very clear, as clear as possible, that life at this moment was a conflict between two energies. One is day, one is night. One is good, one is evil. And the balance should be the union between the two of them.

"I honestly feel that this is what cinema and visual art is. In visual art, it's not enough to know why he's wearing a yellow raincoat, or why she's standing in the sunset in orange light. You have to feel it. Through the use of color, what I was trying to do with the other collabora-

tors was help the story be clear. If you remove the soundtrack for a moment, you can know and recognize these images and understand much more clearly what the story is about."

The strong, straightforward images of "Dick Tracy" speak for themselves. No punches pulled. "Comic-book art," theorized Storaro, "is usually done with very simple and primitive ideas and emotions. They usually use all the symbols that can tell in a very direct way the story and the emotion of the story.

"We were trying to use elements from the original Chester Gould drawings. One of the elements is that the story is usually told in vignette. So what we tried to do is never move the camera at all. Never. Try to make everything work into the frame." This was another bold leap from business-as-usual photography. "Camera movement is normally your grammar in telling the story. In this case we were trying to use a camera that was steady all the time." Storaro's lens became the eye of a hurricane, one image after another swirling in and out of the frame, colliding, exploding, propelling the action.

The size of the frame itself became a subject of hot debate. Standard Hollywood logic dictates that a major motion picture such as *Dick Tracy* be shot for the wide-screen. But that would have bloated the visual image far beyond its comic-strip origins. It was finally determned that a tighter frame, a standard aspect ration of 1.85:1 (1.85 times as wide as it is high; a

The cops await a confrontation with Big Boy's gang, soaked in the bloody light that foreshadows the scene.

The Kid escapes Tracy's apartment in a fireburst of reds and yellows. The red colors of the Kid and the yellows of Tracy pair up the ideas of danger and control.

wide-screen format is 2.35:1), would come closer to duplicating the presentation of the original comic strip.

Chester Gould did not design *Dick Tracy* in a vacuum. His comic strip was born at a time of bizarre artistic ferment. Storaro spotted the influence of certain postexpressionist painters: The mordant depravity of Otto Dix; the crazed sketches of George Grosz, who once called his art an "organized use of insanity to express contempt for a bankrupt world." The twisted visions of Conrad Muller also left their fingerprints on Gould's illustrations.

These painters, remarked Storaro, "seem to have impressed on Chester Gould's mind a melancholy motif: the fascination of evil. Like a true poet of the demonic," Gould drew "figures that people our nightmares. Insatiably cruel, abominably misshapen, they take on the form of evil."

To Storaro, characters like Flattop, Pruneface, and Mumbles were "an exaggeration of reality. This is typical of the art of the era. Gould was putting on the faces of the characters so much characterization to tell the nightmare of the night, to tell how these people were the terrible instincts of the human being, and the evil that is inside. It would be hard to find people whose faces would tell you these kinds of things. That's why, right away, the idea came for prosthetics."

From the mind's eye to the camera lens is the longest trip in Tinseltown. Photographing those villainous prosthetics, lighting a nightmare reality of false faces, promised to be a grinding challenge. Less ambitious filmmakers figure out the easiest way to light a prosthetic and stick to that formula throughout the film. But Storaro's artistic visions required a rainbow of lighting changes, "depending on the dramaturgy of the scene."

For prosthetics designer John Caglione, Storaro built a special mirror with different colored lighting. White, orange, blue. "Very warm light. Very cold light." This enable Caglione to test his prosthetics under a kaleidoscope of effects and plan the necessary adjustments before actual filming began. Close collaboration and a meticulous eye for detail resulted in a spectacular rogues gallery. In *Dick Tracy*, the bad guys really look horrific.

Through the near-hallucinatory use of color and prosthetics, "the audience has to understand right away that we are leading them into a special world. It's not connected to reality." If a matte shot looks like a painting, "it's okay. The movie is inspired by a drawing. The matte paintings have to be done in a style that will remind the audience that this is not a realistic world."

In early discussions with Warren Beatty and costume designer Milena Canonero, "we saw a way to visualize *Dick Tracy*, not only through the use of primary colors, but also by the stylistic connection of art direction, costuming, and photography. Also we can put on top a type of dramatic weight inspired by postexpressionist paintings."

Green and blue overlap—the cops belong to Big Boy—when the Kid hitches a ride.

Colored gels in the windows accented the comic-strip look of Storaro's lighting.

As Tracy drops onto the "teeter-totter" in the Club Ritz attic, the camera catches him in a balletlike pose.

Of course, the postexpressionists did more than depict conflict. They provoked it. "Looking at their paintings," said Storaro, "I discovered a relationship between the drawings and the politics of the moment." Modern, divisive, confrontational. These were the politics of the postexpressionists. But what truly inspired Storaro were the postexpressionists' defiant tones of drama and color, medium and message uniting in disturbing and unforgettable fashion.

In film, noted Storaro, "color has been used with one kind of light, one kind of tonality, depending on whether you're doing a comedy or a musical and so on." Storaro became intent on bursting that stylistic barrier. "Honestly, I started research into the meaning of color after *Apocalypse Now.*" Photographing *La Luna* for Bernardo Bertolucci deepened Storaro's understanding of the symbolism of color. While shooting *One from the Heart* for Francis Ford Coppola at the now-legendary Zoetrope Studios, Storaro experimented with several lighting systems. He finally hit upon a technology, designed by Trend Stage Lighting of Los Angeles, that had been used in stage productions and live television. When *Dick Tracy* came calling, Storaro was ready to shoot the works.

"I had always been looking for a way to use lights to express myself freely, the way I would like to. I literally painted with light every single street on the picture. The streets change color depending on, sequence by

The Club Ritz entrance, oozing purple onto the streets.

Al Pacino, as Big Boy Caprice, takes the low road with Glenne Headly as his hostage.

In a jail cell, Tracy divides a composition of light and shadow.

sequence, character by character, what's happening in the story." Truly, this is where Storaro's genius came to the fore. His streets vibrated with color. Yet he was somehow able to keep the buildings on those streets glowing a ghostly white. Colored gels in the place of building windows enhanced the effect. Eye-popping shots were commonplace. A pink-lit puddle on a blue-lit street is a flat-out impossibility for most cinematographers. For Vittorio Storaro, no problem.

In 1981, Storaro won an Academy Award for his stunning cinematography on *Reds*. The director, who also won the Oscar, was Warren Beatty. "It's amazing the way his mind works," Storaro said of Beatty. "He is so concentrating all the time, that we speak very little on the set during shooting. We always have our tests and our discussions during preproduction.

"For Warren, everything is in connection to the character. He is facing the scene from the inside, from the character's point of view. It's hard for him to see the story told by somebody else, from an author, from a director, from somebody who's not into the scene itself. So it's being shot in an entirely different way than Coppola or Bertolucci shoot their films. And what is fascinating for me is to know different methods, and to know different faces of the same reality."

Initially, Beatty suggested Storaro create a visual feeling akin to the corrupt and decadent atmosphere of Bertolt Brecht's *Threepenny Opera*. "I thought that was a great idea. I did a lot of research about that period. At that time, I didn't understand what kind of connection a comic strip could have with the *Threepenny Opera*. Storaro quickly realized that Brecht's famous work was heavily influenced by the art of the day, which drew him to the postexpressionists, which finally led him back to Chester Gould and the original comic strip, the motherlode of inspiration.

"Of course, the *Dick Tracy* movie is not exactly a transfer of the "Dick Tracy" cartoon, because they are two different art forms. Our picture is inspired by the comic strip, but it has to be something original, something different. It has to be a movie.

"We spent a lot of energy in the design and in doing the film. We think it's really an original piece of work."

A stark graphic image illustrates the extremes of contrast in Storaro's lighting.

COSTUME DESIGN
and
"No grief for the man?"
"I'm wearing black underwear."
or
FIBER-EXPERT
CANONERO TO TESTIFY

Candy-colored bad guys display their duds.

When Big Boy Caprice blusters out of police custody howling "False arrest!" to the members of the press, he wears an elegant, if overly large, wool overcoat and homburg. The frame zaps in to a close-up. We see that Big Boy's costly coat has a collar that looks like a *dead sheep*. Gray and grungy, that collar blows his cover, cracks a window onto the evil that stains his soul.

Insights like this one, where the fabric of a character's costume both conceals and reveals the character himself, belong to *Dick Tracy* costume designer Milena Canonero.

As she does on all her films, Canonero, along with Warren Beatty, supervised the "look" of the characters in *Dick Tracy*—makeup and hair, as well as costumes. In deciding how *Tracy*'s denizens of the Sunday comics could be metamorphosed into citizens of cinema, she began with basic research, first reading up on Tracy's creator, Chester Gould.

She sought out avenues into Gould's psyche and grew fascinated with his righteous law-abiding politics and his nightmarish representations of evil. She came to understand the comic artist's clear-cut delineations

Two-time Academy Award winner for Best Costumes (Barry Lyndon and Chariots of Fire), Milena Canonero.

between right and wrong, and the nature of the violence, "the hot-lead route," that guided his heroes in their conquest of his villains.

Canonero clipped original comic-strip drawings of all the characters that were in the movie, had them photographed, blown up, and tacked to a bulletin board for reference in creating makeup, hair, and wardrobe. The costume designer realized that her task in *Dick Tracy* was not to duplicate the comic strip, but to interpret it for movie audiences by dressing it up in images more suited to modern eyes.

She also made certain that her ideas on outfitting the characters jibed with Warren Beatty's vision of the movie. "Warren is very aware that sometimes a look can

Big Boy in an expensive overcoat with a slush-colored collar.

carry the film away from the audience, so you have to balance that. On the other hand, this film was also very much about a look. The characters are stereotypes, so their originality depended on how we presented them," Canonero explained. "If you look at the original color comic strips, they're simplistic. The ones from 1930 to the early forties use four, five, sometimes six colors. I tried to make the characters a little more interesting in the hair, the makeup, the ties—however I could."

At Beatty's direction, Canonero narrowed her palette of costume colors to ten basics: red, fuchsia, orange, yellow, green, blue, plum, cyan, black, and white. Every time a blue appeared on a costume, it was the same blue. Every yellow she used was "Dick Tracy Yellow." "With the way materials react to color and light, it may seem that there are nuances, but in fact there are just those ten. No browns, no midtones, no grays," Canonero pointed out.

Once the colors had been finalized, she gave Richard Sylbert's art department sample swatches of each fabric color, so that the color of the clothes would match precisely the color of the sets. If Sylbert wanted a piece of furniture in green, he would use the same color fabric as the green in Canonero's costumes. The idea of using a limited palette of primary colors had come from the comic strip, but the artistic principles at work here sprang from Warren Beatty and Vittorio Storaro's research into German postexpressionist art of the late 1930s.

Postexpressionism was characterized by an "anti-naturalist" style, which used intensified colors and simplified forms to define man's relationship to his environment. "Dick Tracy," after all, depicted a man trying to define his relationship to the crime-ridden world in which he lived—an expressionist kind of storyline. Simplicity and intensity became the watchwords of Canonero and all the film's creators. As they sought to express themselves on the blank canvas of the screen, a continual exchange of information—fabric swatches, research articles, photographs, phone calls, faxes, storyboards, conceptual art, script notes—became the life's blood of this brand-new idea for designing the look of a movie.

Canonero's research also refreshed her with the fashions of the period—the tendencies and trends, the silhouettes, the types of hats, coats, and gloves. "It's not that you go back to school," she remarked, "there's no time for that. But you prepare your research so that when you start designing the costumes, you don't do a 1990 version of 1939. I hate that in a movie. I like to do period costumes, anyway."

She found that *Dick Tracy* would be set in a time of transition for fashion, with the influence of the forties already apparent and the styles of the thirties still popular. Skirts were inching their way up, but weren't yet what you'd call short. Shoulders were getting bigger, but weren't padded in the extreme. Women's

The cat on her way to "eat her canary."

The silver-lamé number for "More" was a trial for Canonero, but lit up Breathless like the Moon.

The inviting front of Breathless's dress delivers a message to Tracy. The zigzag back tells the audience she can't escape bondage to the bad life.

Western's custom-made women's costume department, Tzetzi (SET-see) Ganev, had needled and threaded some of Hollywood's greatest stars—Barbara Stanwyck, Bette Davis, Jane Fonda, Ingrid Bergman, Marlene Dietrich—and now it was Madonna's turn.

"When Madonna was there getting fitted, Tzetzi used to tell us stories about the actresses who stood for hours while they were fitted. Marlene Dietrich, for one dress, stood there for twelve hours while everything was stitched on her. I think maybe telling these stories was a way for Tzetzi to tell Madonna that she shouldn't be so much in a hurry to go to her next meeting. Madonna was wonderful, but she's a very busy lady, who's always doing a lot of things. Tzetzi was always trying to keep her a little longer if possible, and entertain her with all these stories," Canonero said with a smile.

For Madonna's *femme fatale* character Breathless Mahoney, Canonero cloaked the actress/singer primarily in black, the color of the night. She originally had planned to go heavy on veils and hats for Madonna. "I wanted the audience to realize that Breathless always lived behind a mask or veil of some kind or other. But Warren preferred to see her face." The costume designer was not surprised. "You work on ideas like this in preproduction, then it comes to practical terms, when you come to see what the director likes more about the character." Beatty—who could argue?—liked Breathless's face and her body, and wanted the costumes to leave these obvious assets on display. Milena's millinery would have to wait for another movie.

Because she found the 1930s styles cut a clearer picture of Breathless's mobster-moll sexuality, Canonero came to think of her as a dame whose clothing budget ran ahead of her fashion sense. Canonero stayed away from the sharper silhouettes of the forties, "which would have made Breathless more fashionable for a woman of the period, but would have given her a harder look." Instead she chose a silhouette that "made her look more like a snake, more like a sleek animal." The shoulders were natural, the hair was tousled and curly.

When Breathless tries to seduce Dick Tracy in his office, she appears in a cape with a leopard-skin collar, and underneath, an invitingly décolleté dress with crisscross lacing on a low-cut back. No dialogue was necessary. This costume is what the scene is all about. The leopard-skin collar gave it a feline feel—Breathless is the cat who plans on eating her yellow canary. At the same time, the laces across the back of the dress

hairstyles had not yet become the graphic and powerful Joan Crawfordish look of the forties, but remained a little bit Carol Lombardy, with finger waves and curls. The designer had a lot of leeway.

Except for fifty tuxedos that were rented for a scene in the Club Ritz, Canonero designed and created all the costumes for the film. After completing her research and making thumbnail sketches for each of the characters, she began looking for the right fabric for each costume. She worked exclusively with natural fabrics— "I never use synthetics, and besides, we would have to dye nearly every piece of material we used, and synthetic materials are next to impossible to dye."

Setting up her headquarters in the big fitting room a Hollywood's legendary Western Costume Company, Canonero brought in the cast for fittings. The head of

Canonero clothed Bug Bailey in the colors of a bumblebee.

The beautiful and intricate stitching on Estelle Parsons's costume registers an expression that matches the one on her face.

indicate that she's a prisoner, in love with a man she can never have, jailed by a life she cannot escape. For Canonero, every costume makes a statement that underscores the context of the scene.

Beatty's primary concern with Madonna's costumes was that they fit her like a glove, accenting the curves of her body, and that the dresses she wore for the nightclub numbers gave her the freedom to move and

dance. Canonero sometimes found these two design criteria at cross-purposes. "Sometimes it was difficult to get all to click together," she said. "If I made the dress to fit tightly, it didn't give her the freedom of movement. If it was fitted to give her freedom of movement, it didn't have the shape that we wanted, and it was a problem keeping up the décolletage."

Like the moon, Breathless Mahoney only comes out at night. Canonero created one moon-colored costume for Breathless's nightclub number "More" during the film's last scene at the Club Ritz. The silver-lamé dress nearly turned into the costumer's Waterloo. When she saw it on the set under Storaro's lavender-and-blue lighting, the silver disappeared and it looked like a *white* dress. She decided to dye it a shade of gray that would make the silver come out more strongly under the light. "It was this beautiful original silver lamé," lamented Canonero, "which you can't find anywhere, because they don't make it anymore. When we dyed it, it became loose, like chewing gum. When we started shooting, I almost died, because everything was pulling one way and the other. Tzetzi worked all day and night at Western Costume with her sewing assistant, and we tried to mold it to Madonna's body. So it worked, but I don't think I'll be dyeing any more silver lamé."

In most instances, Canonero anticipated the effect that Storaro's lighting would have on the costumes and expected that lighting to enliven her handicraft for its appearance on the screen. "I didn't want my colors to stay exactly as they were. Vittorio put layers on what I was creating, so that it would come out as something else, and not so plain and placid and dull as the primary colors Dick Sylbert and I were doing. It gives the movie another great ingredient.

"We all had long conversations before we started, but in the end we all did our bit and the whole thing coincides. Sometimes a color that is red as you prepare it turns mauve before the light, and now and again you see the original color. It comes out of the light and you see the red. It moves. Otherwise you end up with a 1950s musical, or a comic strip, and we wanted to give it more substance."

The actors in *Dick Tracy* trusted Canonero's proven instincts, with Beatty restraining her on occasions when the costumes bordered on the kind of busyness that would get in the way of an audience's sympathy, or a character's humanity. Canonero could have gone over the top with the two girls, Breathless and Tess. In the "Tracy" comic strips, Tess Trueheart was "a real fashion

A pinstriped, bulked-up, greased-down nut case.

plate, always dressed to the nines in outfits that were frilly and cute." In the movie, Canonero made it more simple: "She's got two changes of clothes. She has a job and she goes with a detective, so she doesn't have much money. Even though she's stylish, it wouldn't make sense in the movie that suddenly she's running riot with all these changes, and all these little fashion gizmos. So I kept it simple because that was Warren's mandate. But within that, there's a style, because we want the audience to like her."

For the first part of the film, Tess Trueheart wears a green dress, which, in the film's color scheme, suggests tranquillity, a sense of order. Her job at the florist surrounds her with the greens of nature. In the second half of the film, when things heat up and Big Boy ensnares her in his kidnapping-and-extortion plot, she's dressed in red, which the filmmakers frequently used to indicate danger.

Miss Trueheart's budget-conscious wardrobe also includes a hat shaped, appropriately enough, like a heart. Canonero didn't pluck this idea out of thin air—hearts were a popular motif of the era, commonly seen on brooches and embroidery.

The color of danger also clothed the most dangerous character in the film, Al Pacino's Big Boy Caprice. Canonero's styling of Big Boy began in makeup, where she collaborated with makeup designers John Caglione and Doug Drexler to bring out both the crook and comedian in Pacino. "It was wonderful working with Al. We had sessions sometimes for seven or eight hours in the big dressing room at Western, where he would try different prosthetics on his face, and different pieces of clothing, so that he could actually invent his character—how he talked, how he moved. That was quite exciting, a real one-man show. When Al started improvising, he would come up with such funny lines! I didn't realize he had such a sense of humor.

"Sometimes actors don't bring you too much," she said, "but we really worked together with Al to try to get to his character. We tried all kinds of shapes of suits and coats. We built up his body, padded the shoulders, the stomach, gave him a big rear end. Big Boy shows affluence in his clothes. They are too big, they don't fit, but his coats have fur collars. He's the only one in the picture who had pinstriped suits. And he has all the watch chains and accessories, but basically you can see that underneath he's a slob. We let his hair flow slightly longer, but greasy, dirty, because he's a vicious man and he plays dirty games. So he has all the fashionable clothes, the homburg, but it all points to an air of respectability completely gone wrong."

On the theory that bad guys always dress better than good guys, perhaps because they have more to hide, Big Boy's henchmen were a vogue bunch of rogues. Bill Forsythe, the actor who portrayed Flattop, would always strike and hold a pose, hands in pockets, confrontational, unmovable. Canonero gave him a well-defined silhouette with a dapper double-breasted purple suit that was a tad too tight. His chokingly thin bow tie accented the size and flatness of his head. Mindful that he was the film's number-one killer, she topped him off with a black overcoat so the look wouldn't get too buoyant.

Itchy, who cackles with an oddball laugh, reminded Milena of a crazy fox. She dressed him in a royal-blue suit, with a black shirt to suggest the world of shadows and darkness inhabited by the character. His laugh, his distended nose, and crooked smile led her to assign him a funny little tie and a tie bar with an arrow—the

Flattop's thin bow tie accentuated the size and flatness of his head.

Seymour Cassel's comfortable Sam Catchem, a baggy-clothes cop.

arrow because she felt that "his laughter had a piercing quality, capable of puncturing holes in people. I found some ties of the period that had beautiful graphic designs on them. Dick Tracy's tie was easy. In the comic strip, he always wore a striped tie, and that's what he wore in the film. But on the other characters one color would have been boring, so we really went to town with the ties."

Littleface, the mobster with the gargantuan head and diminutive features, was a tricky character to outfit, for obvious reasons. Trickiest of all was his fedora, which was roughly the size of a coffee table. "A hat that big, you can't block it," said Canonero, referring to the traditional way in which hats are manufactured. "I made several prototypes in foam. Then we molded over it a stiff mesh netting, which you can steam and shape. To this we stitched the felt fabric. I chose black as the color of the hat so the stitching wouldn't show. The other characters around him are all wearing hats, so if we got the proportions wrong, it would really stand out. The proportions were very tricky.

"You don't invent clothing, you play with silhouette, colors, and styles to reflect the character. For instance, the character of Bug Bailey. Bug to me was a bug, he was an insect. And in the movie, he's bugging Big Boy. So I made him yellow and black. He's one of the men who belongs to Dick Tracy, so his jacket is one of the typical American jackets of the period, the two-toned material, yellow with little black-and-yellow checks. The sleeves are black, the back is black. And he wears a cap instead of a hat. A little bit of a bug."

Sam Catchem and Pat Patton also belonged to the Tracy team, so Canonero dressed Pat in a green suit, and Sam in orange, colors she labels as "kind" and "gentle." To Pat's wardrobe she added a yellow-and-white bow tie as an emblem of his allegiance to Tracy. The silhouettes of their suits are slouchy and comfortable looking, hewing to her idea that cops aren't as concerned with fashion as crooks.

When nine-year-old Charlie Korsmo, who starred as the Kid, arrived for his costume fitting, Canonero had trouble at first envisioning him as the street urchin of the film's script. He had a delicacy about his features that ran contrary to her idea of the character, and she didn't hold back from telling Beatty. "Warren is terrific about his casting, because he always shows you the people he's interested in. He makes you feel that he wants you to have an opinion—not so much about his choice in casting, but to get a reaction."

She understood that Beatty cast young Charlie because of his acting ability—he was brilliant in his screen test—and because of his tremendous intelligence—which meant that he could take direction. Beatty puts a lot of stock in intelligence. So she figured out a way to make Korsmo's physical frailty work to his advantage in portraying the Kid.

First, she gave him a haircut. A *bad* haircut. "His hair was limp, blondish, not that interesting, so we cut it a little bit shaggily, we dyed it red, and put freckles on his face. He's got two outfits. The first is the street clothes, poor, slightly big, so they show how skinny he is, and to make him look like he's not eating a lot. Most of the other kids that Warren tested were terribly healthy. You couldn't imagine that they'd have a difficult time finding food, and that they have to steal for a living. With Charlie, that was not the problem. So I made his clothes bigger than they should have been, like he stole them or somebody gave them to him. I tried to use two specific colors for the first outfit—dark, towards black; and orange."

When Tess and Tracy take the Kid under their wing, they buy him a red jacket and black trousers. The combination of colors came, as usual, out of the underlying logic of the movie's design. The black pants suggested a connection with Tracy and his black suit, and also indicated that the Kid was not yet out of the shadow world, that he had not completely escaped his experiences on the street. The red jacket sprang from the idea that every time the audience sees the Kid, he's caught up in some traumatic activity—running, or being chased, saving Dick Tracy or escaping danger. Whether or not the audience would pick up on these connections did not concern Canonero. She wasn't trying to telegraph the story, but rather to develop a scheme for her own designs that would support, and not contradict, the story Beatty was telling. "You've got to have these explanations for yourself. Otherwise, you get very confused," she said with a sigh.

There were no explanations necessary for the garb of the film's title character. Dick Tracy wore a yellow raincoat and hat, and a black suit with a red tie. Always had. Canonero and Beatty both knew enough not to tamper with half a century of tradition. Simple, right? Not if the costumer and star are perfectionists.

Creating Tracy's raincoat and hat was nearly as tricky as spinning straw into gold. Canonero found the material she wanted—a heavy gabardine wool with a slight rib, a cloth with the proper substance and weight for

The Kid's red coat flashes in and out of the picture like a warning light.

Tracy—in England. She could not, however, find it in yellow, only white, so it was back once more to the old dyeing board. She tried several raincoats of the period on Beatty, until she found a style of double-breasted coat with a silhouette she liked. Then she dyed large swatches of the gabardine in seven different variations of yellow and draped these over Beatty, who was dressed in a black off-the-rack suit. Beatty decided which of the seven yellows he liked best, and Canonero checked with Vittorio Storaro to make certain that the yellow wouldn't shift too far up or down the color spectrum under his lighting. She then had a prototype of the coat made by a tailor at Universal Studios and took this prototype to Burberry's in New York to have it duplicated.

"When the people at Burberry's saw it, they freaked out," she said laughing. "They said, 'Oh God, we hope you're doing the right thing. Does it have to be that

A busy backstage before a Club Ritz scene. In addition to costumes, Canonero supervised the styling of makeup and hair.

Canonero with director of photography Vittorio Storaro.

yellow? Does it have to be that strong?' I assured them that they'd like it. And I was looking in a fashion magazine the other day and I see now that everybody's doing these colors." Even in fashion, it seems, Dick Tracy can do no wrong.

With the raincoat in the wardrobe closet, the costumer moved on to the detective's familiar hat. When Chester Gould decided to top off Tracy with a yellow fedora, little did he know what kind of headache he'd be causing Milena Canonero sixty years later.

"It's very, very difficult to make a man's hat in such a delicate color. You need a special dye and you need to make many, many hats before you get enough out of the group that are perfect. We had to use a white felt, and white felt which is completely clean and pure hardly exists. You have to use a man's felt. If you used a woman's felt, the hat would look like a horrible cheap little camp thing."

Canonero contacted the folks at Stetson, deep in the heart of Texas, who turned out dozens and dozens of yellow fedoras. Out of a batch of twenty, they would produce four or five that met her demanding specifications. The prototypes had three different sizes of crowns, three different sizes of brims, and all the combinations thereof. Beatty was photographed in screen tests with each of the hats.

"At some point, you become terribly confused," she admitted. "You don't know anymore what you are doing." Let's see . . . the high crown with the short brim, or the short crown with the long brim, or the medium crown with the medium brim, or the . . . ? They finally decided on the high crown with the medium brim.

Tracy's costume would not be complete without certain trademark tools of the law enforcement trade. Property Master C. J. Maguire outfitted the detective with a two-way wrist radio copied from the 1931 comic strip in which it first appeared. The watch template (which actually worked) and the radio (which didn't) were manufactured by Ian Campbell, a jeweler from Santa Clarita, California. Maguire had a set of ten on hand for the filming. The only difference between the film version of the wrist radio and the one

the actors to wear their emotions, literally, on their sleeves.

She would prefer that people not dwell on the filmographic details of her career. "Just say I'm Milena Canonero and that I've done lots of films," she advised. What? Forget that she started her film career designing costumes for Stanley Kubrick on *A Clockwork Orange*? Have flannels ever been so frightening as they were in *The Shining*, or satins so exquisite as in *Barry Lyndon*, for which she won an Academy Award? Has a movie ever gotten more mileage out of college boys in their underwear than the one which won Canonero her second Oscar, *Chariots of Fire*?

Has a costume designer ever said so much with so few colors as Milena Canonero did in *Dick Tracy*? Forget? Not a chance. These are threads to remember.

Tess Trueheart's hat was an actual style of the 1930s.

Tracy's yellow ensemble outlined Beatty in strong primary colors. The coat is by Burberry, the hat by Stetson.

that appeared in the comic strip was the wrist antenna, which ran up the detective's sleeve in the comics, but was omitted from the film.

Tracy's badge was modeled on the Chicago Police badges of the thirties and made generic for the film. His gun was a Colt pocket model .32 caliber, which was convenient, easy to hold, and popular with police detectives of the thirties. Maguire had the butt of the gun engraved with Tracy's name, as he did with Tracy's pen-and-pencil set, detail touches that would not be noticed by audiences, but that helped give Beatty as an actor an aura of Dick Tracy's reality and his completeness as a character.

Everyone who works on a movie is in the business of telling a story. Scriptwriters do it with words. Actors do it with emotions. A costume designer does it with fabric. One got the crazy notion in *Dick Tracy* that these costumes were not actually made of cloth, but that somehow Milena Canonero had found a way for

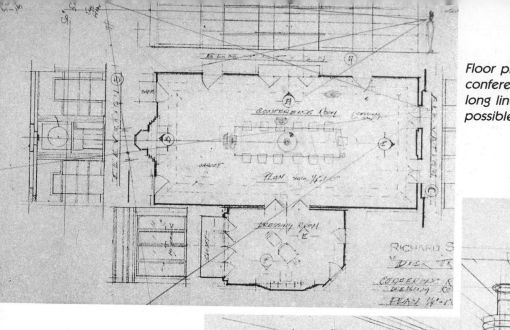

Floor plans and elevations for Big Boy's conference room upstairs of the Club Ritz. The long lines angling across the drawing indicate possible camera setups.

PRODUCTION DESIGN
and
"This is a private club, copper. You got a membership card?"
or
SYLBERT DESIGN PLANS UNVEILED

"There's a world of hummers out there," remarked *Dick Tracy* production designer Richard Sylbert as he laid out the elaborate plans and sketches for the film on a coffee table in his Hollywood apartment, unveiling clue after clue to *Tracy*'s radical visual style. "It's like Mozart saying I've got this idea for music, but I don't know how to play the piano. *You* play the piano and I'll hum."

Richard Sylbert is no hummer. He composes his de- signs and orchestrates their production with the skill of one of Hollywood's true maestros. His credits—from the cloistered macabre of *Rosemary's Baby* to the sunny *noir* of *Chinatown* to the globe-girdling look of *Reds*—demonstrate not only his range as a designer, but the reliance that directors such as Roman Polanski and Warren Beatty place upon him to create an ambience for their films.

There has never been a better proof of the old artistic axiom "less is more" than in the production design of *Dick Tracy*. The colors of the sets and costumes, like the emotions of the characters, are primary. The architecture, like the division between Good and Evil, is clean, well defined, drawn in straight lines. The result is that

Bill Major, working from Sylbert's penciled designs, drew color art of the conference room.

The conference room. Sylbert designed it in the black-and-red of the Nazi flag, and felt a warm glow when he saw that Pacino's Big Boy was a takeoff on Hitler.

Bill Major's drawing of the diner. Originally, Tracy and Tess would discover the Kid asleep in a booth.

The diner scene in the film. Big blocks of color and texture embolden the design and frame the Kid, who has now become the focus of the scene, having just stolen a watch.

Dick Tracy resonates with meaning in every frame. Everything in the picture, beginning with the production design, defines, without ambiguity, the emotional dynamic of the story. But the lyrical loveliness of this idea was not easily achieved. "It was torture," reflected Sylbert. "Torture in the good sense. We had to beat it out for a long time."

Between 1986 and 1988, Warren Beatty called Sylbert to his Mulholland Drive home several times to sit in the kitchen and discuss *Dick Tracy*. As Sylbert well knew, this was a familiar ritual in Beatty's romances with movie projects. "I've known Warren for twenty-nine years. He's the oldest friend I have in Hollywood. I've done seven pictures with him and I know that when he's ready, he'll be ready. And so, as it did with the nine years for *Reds* and the five years for *Shampoo*, finally it happens. One meeting when you realize you're getting serious."

Bill Major's illustration demonstrating the "less is more" principle.

The hallway as depicted in the film.

That one meeting took place early in 1988, with Beatty, cinematographer Vittorio Storaro, costume designer Milena Canonero, and Sylbert. In the high-stakes poker game of film production, this is the kind of hand Beatty was looking to bet on. Storaro had researched the subject of Dick Tracy meticulously, through the color comic-strip art he had found in San Francisco, and in books on the art of the period he'd unearthed in Europe. The period. What period? That

became one of the first questions they had to answer.

Beatty decided to shift the time period from 1928 to "1930–late," steering it away from the twenties styles altogether and keeping it ahead of the war years. This had two crucial ramifications on the design of the film: It pointed to a streamlined look that was coming into being at that time—in art, in design, and in the way women looked—and it guided them toward postexpressionist art as a source of inspiration.

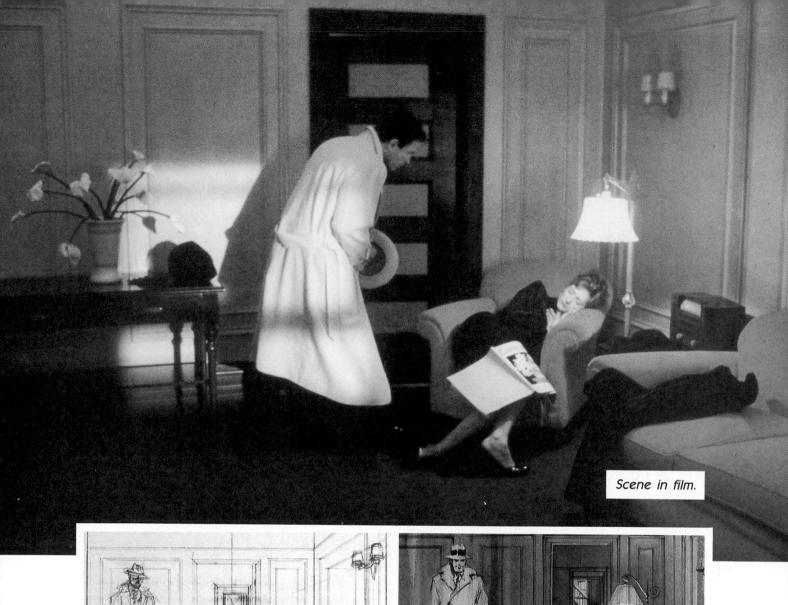

Scene in film.

Sylbert's pencil sketch to show possible camera projection for scene.

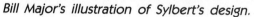

Bill Major's illustration of Sylbert's design.

Streamlined deco designs . . . bold colors . . . grotesque images . . . a guy in a yellow raincoat— there seemed to be a unifying design in there somewhere, and it was Richard Sylbert's job to lay the cornerstones.

Nothing in his past experience had prepared Sylbert for what lay ahead. "There was something about this picture that we knew was going to be a serious obstacle," continued Sylbert. This was a world that he had

to design from scratch, and "all the things that Vittorio, Milena, and myself had done through the years got us nowhere, except that your own instinct is still your instinct. All the things that we did for other movies did not count. Those were specific, and we weren't doing specific, we were doing generic. There was no existing world. We couldn't go with Warren to Chicago and do a movie in a real world, a specific world, because this guy's got a yellow hat and raincoat, and the only thing

"The biggest car anybody had ever seen."

A generic taxi.

Itchy's car.

we'd get right is the hat and raincoat! We wouldn't have been making *Dick Tracy*."

They got there the hard way, which was that "nobody knew for sure. We were all scared to death, because this time, the only way to win was by failing. When you throw all your experience away, and I mean *away*, you don't know how you're going to do it, you *learn* how to it."

Using the original Chester Gould color comic strip as his "bible," or visual reference guide, Sylbert first began thinking about how to design the "generic cars" Warren Beatty had requested for the film. In a normal film set in the late thirties, the production designer can use one car from 1937, one from 1927, one from 1935—he has ten or fifteen years to tool around with. They all fit. Beatty realized that cars of a specific make or model would not be true to the laws of Chester Gould's comics. The cars in the movie belong to Dick Tracy's

Flattop's car. It was Beatty's idea to "genericize" cars like all the other icons in the film. Except to hard-core car buffs, the make and year of each auto was indecipherable.

world alone, and not to an identifiable motor company or model year. There would be, the production designer decided, only two "types" of cars in *Dick Tracy*—good guy cars and gangster cars. "The gangster cars are bigger."

The next step in homing in on *Tracy*'s world was to restrict the number of colors in the film by first restricting the number of colors used in costuming. "It's the logical way to begin. Costumes are more important than walls. After all, in a movie, an actor can fill the entire screen—this much of him," explained Sylbert, framing himself in a medium close-up. "And a swatch of fabric doesn't cost that much money to look at." At each production meeting, Beatty wiped more and more colors off the palette until only seven primary colors, plus black and white, remained. Red, orange, yellow, green, blue, indigo, and violet—does the name Roy G. Biv ring a bell?

"Now we were talking about a real idea here, and *simplicity*," said Sylbert. "The more we did, the more courage we got." One day early in preproduction, Sylbert accompanied Beatty to the backlot at Universal Studios, where the two of them took a walk down New York Street, as Sylbert made a request he had never before made of a director. "I said, 'You don't have any choice, Warren. You can't make this picture in a city. Don't even think about it.'"

Sylbert had designed over forty movies, and in that time worked on a studio backlot only once, and that was for only one shot in *Chinatown*. He despised the "backlot look," and yet he knew that on this picture it would work in his favor. "If you're going to do *Dick Tracy* there's only one way to do it, and that's with icons, where a car is just a car and a building is just a building. A backlot is nothing but a series of icons—of a city or a village or a town, whatever. Most of the backlots are gone. Universal and the Burbank Studios are the only ones that have anything left. But even that was interesting, because the less there was of that, the better off we were going to be, because we knew from the beginning that the outside world would be painted with mattes."

With most of the theorizing behind him, Sylbert got to work. He began by sketching nine exterior scenes in charcoal and ink. These were done to establish the mood of the movie, ninety percent of which took place at night. He turned the sketches over to production illustrator Leon Harris, a longtime collaborator, who took them the next step up the evolutionary ladder.

A Sylbert charcoal-and-ink conceptual sketch. Note the rain and the softly silhouetted buildings in the background. In the finished design there was "no atmosphere"—they eliminated the weather, and the background mattes stayed in sharp focus all the way to the horizon.

The Club Ritz under construction.

Bill Major's production drawing for Tracy's entrance at the Club Ritz.

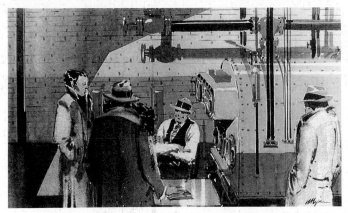

Bill Major's art of the boiler-room scene.

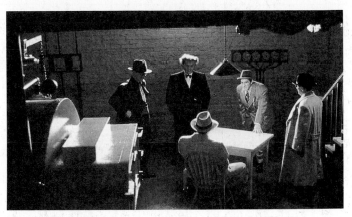

The boiler-room scene, reverse angle of Major's production drawing.

In the preliminary sketches by Sylbert and Harris, a generic city looms over Steve the Tramp's shack; Tracy chases the Kid past a long warehouse labeled simply "WAREHOUSE"; the wheels of a steam locomotive blast past the camera; a railroad yard becomes a series of geometric designs; the monuments in a cemetery blend into the buildings of the city in the background, so that the two are indistinguishable; an Industrial Age drawbridge spans a river lined with rotting wooden docks. This was the shadowy world of *Dick Tracy*, the gritty city where the gumshoe would leave his footprint.

Many of the ideas conveyed by the preliminary art spilled over into the film: The generic labeling of products and places, the suggestion of danger lurking in the maw of the city, the images of corrupted innocence.

A warehouse, as conceived by Sylbert.

With these sketches, Sylbert began establishing a set of ideas that would become rules of design for the hundreds of people who would eventually work to make *Tracy*'s world whole. Illustrator Harris drew two scenes in color—one to establish the indigo mood of the night, the other to communicate the yellow of sunrise over the city. Harris's drawings also became the preliminary layouts for the fifty mattes that would be needed in the film.

"Those layouts were important," Sylbert pointed out, "because in production, certain commitments to color and lighting were made. We designed shots in which the lower right-hand corner was real, the rest was fake." That commitment often called for a lot of artistic courage, because the filmmakers knew they were pushing the color envelope on this one. "The mattes that were eighty percent live-action were easy. Those that were twenty percent live-action are tough. The stuff we did at first paid off enormously, because we had one more chance in postproduction to make the movies better. We were learning things about this world right through to the end."

Tracy's entrance at the Club Ritz. Danger awaits!

The sets on the backlot functioned as what Sylbert called the "half-sized world." The street in front of the Club Ritz, the street in front of Tess Trueheart's apartment, the street Tracy lived on—these and most exterior sets the actor, and the audience's relationship to the actor, were what Sylbert referred to as a "human distance." Everything beyond that human distance was painted. *Dick Tracy* is quite possibly the first motion picture in which mattes were not used to complete an illusion of reality, but to *become* the look of the movie, a look somewhere between reality and fantasy.

Sylbert next turned his focus to the fifty-three interiors he would have to design, beginning with the largest and most complex set, the Club Ritz nightclub. It would be nearly the last set utilized in the production, but because of its size, it would influence everything else he did. "You always do the biggest set first. You know you're going to be in it longer than anywhere else, and if you're going to spend money, you might as well spend it on that." Once he had designed the nightclub, he moved on to what was above it, which was Big Boy's conference room, and then the attic above that (where Bug Bailey sets up his bugging operation), and then the rooftop.

Characterized by its art-deco opulence, the Club Ritz had four entrances, like entryways from locker rooms, from which teams of good guys and bad guys would emerge to compete, with Breathless Mahoney on display like a trophy at center court. Storaro painted the four entrances in different colors, the hues foreshadowing the mood created by a new arrival. The entrance Tracy uses to raid the Club and collar Big Boy was lit in red—danger awaits!

Even before shooting began, some of the fundamental things of the production design began to apply. Sylbert knew that in the late-thirties time frame of the film, the gangsters were taking over the world, not just in Chicago, or in Chester Gould's comic strip. Hitler was coming to power. Mussolini was muscling his way to the top. It was the Age of the Gangster. And so he designed Big Boy Caprice's conference room, his place of business, in red and black—the colors of the Nazi flag.

Al Pacino, meanwhile, was with Milena Canonero and the makeup designers, Caglione and Drexler, creating the character and the look of Big Boy. When Pacino appeared on the set for the first time, Sylbert discov-

The rooftop scene combined a full-sized set (foreground) with a cityscape that was part forced-perspective (background) and part matte-painting (added later).

Big Boy in the gearhouse. By making the floor on one level, Beatty eliminated continuity problems from the scene.

Sylbert's preliminary sketches for the gearhouse scene.

ered to his delight that the actor had chosen to play Big Boy as a Hitlerized comic-book mobster. A Nazi knucklehead. "There's an example of two people getting the same answer from the same problem in different ways," commented Sylbert. The design of the movie seemed to be speaking everyone's language.

With the Club Ritz embedded in his brain, Sylbert cranked out plans for the smaller sets in the picture. Because of the quantity of work involved in designing and overseeing the construction of fifty-three sets, Sylbert worked quickly in pencil, drawing plans and

elevations that he would turn over to art director Harold Michelson, production illustrator Bill Major, and set designer James Murakami. To the layman, his sketches were abstractions of altitude and angle. To the art department, they housed the secrets of making the movie.

Designing the sets took from June 13, 1988 to the first day of shooting, February 2, 1989. "I started alone and did all the things I could do by myself, then brought Harold Michelson in," recalled Sylbert. "He's the best art director in California, and he's worked with me off and on for twenty-five years. I made him an art director on *Catch 22* because I needed his experience on that picture—he was a bombardier in World War II."

Michelson worked out the projections on each exterior shot that required a matte. These projections, by indicating a camera lens and the height of the lens off the ground, calculated exactly what portion of the frame would be composed of the actual set and what would be painted as a matte. Michelson also worked out projections for the bridge and railroad scenes, which would combine full-scale sets with models and miniatures.

Sylbert himself worked out projections—calculating what the camera would see—for each interior set. These went along with his penciled plans and elevations, to illustrator Bill Major, who executed watercolor drawings of the sets, and to set designer James Murakami, who drafted detailed quarter-inch-scale blueprints.

The bridge and gearhouse scenes required the most complex staging in the film—the bridge sequence because it called for a miniature, the gearhouse scene because it was full of complex moving parts and called for the final confrontation between Tracy and Big Boy to take place on several levels of flooring. Sylbert had these scenes storyboarded several times. He also built a scale model of the gearhouse, which he showed to Beatty. It was a torture chamber, a German expression-ist torture chamber. "Warren asked if we had to have the different levels. He didn't want them. And you know, he was right. There were a lot of productions decisions that had to be made if you had different levels to the gearhouse, scaffolding and such—which cost money. But that wasn't his primary reason. His primary reason was: These were two titans in a ring. It's a flat ring, a level playing field. The gears   of course, for the mood—but a flat floor. It was the solution to all the production problems, because once we had a flat floor, we weren't concerned with continuity at all. We didn't need storyboards. We were in a boxing ring. Which way did we want to shoot? Any way we wanted, we could."

The Idea Whose Time Had Come—using comic-book colors to conjure up Dick Tracy's world—proved an irresistible force, animating the production, focusing it, coursing through it like a Technicolor current. Sylbert painted portions of the Universal backlot in the colors of the movie. After he'd seen the first day of dailies, he painted more of it. And more. He painted every piece of furniture, every car, painted the streets so no grease spots would show, painted everything in the apartments and offices, painted them the way Chester Gould would have, by accenting them like a Sunday color supplement. He discovered something interesting: If a

Sylbert's design of this setting for The Blank suggested the imprisoned psyche of the character.

The Blank, as drawn by Chester Gould for the comic strip.

scene had Dick Tracy in it, he could "move" Tracy's yellow around the room. Yellow water cooler. Yellow coat. Yellow flower. The same could be done with red, or with green, as with the police station's peaceful green hues.

During preproduction, Sylbert and most of his art department carried swatches of costume cloth around with them. These were, in effect, pocket palettes. All anybody had to say was "Gimme the red" or "Gimme the yellow" and his collaborators would know that the leatherette upholstery in the diner was the same color as Big Boy's suit; that the Formica walls were the same yellow as Tracy's coat, which was also the color of the cabs. "When you're making a generic movie, you really have to be serious about it, because if you keep breaking the rules you set up, you just harm yourself," said Sylbert. "So the control, my favorite phrase, was *dead serious.*"

It had to be dead serious, but that didn't mean it had to be dead-on real. "If it became too realistic, too atmospheric, it wouldn't work. We started out with atmospheric, but we took it out. You couldn't have clouds and fog. You couldn't have things get softer and softer as they got farther away from you." Another feature of the design was that there was never anything allowed on the walls. Only fixtures, such as switch boxes and sconces, only things that were permanent.

"*Dick Tracy* didn't lend itself to the Taj Mahal," Sylbert continued. "It's not supposed to. *Dick Tracy* is about how simple things can be, and how right, if they're minimalized."

Sylbert's early training in 1950s television meant that his preproduction work was well organized. ("You were organized because you had to be. Everything happened fast.") In Sylbert's world, the picture gets designed before the first day of shooting. "Any improvements, fine, we learned on the way. But we were looking to make a picture that was this movie and no other. All these parts belonged in the same picture, they all had a reason for being related to one another. We had to do it beforehand. It wasn't *Chinatown.* That was the real world. If you went outside with the camera, you'd get something back."

The scrupulous planning didn't mean the *Tracy* production design was glitch-free. Occasionally Sylbert had to improvise. On one occasion, he arrived on a set under construction—the City Hall corridor where Tracy confronts District Attorney Fletcher—and saw immediately that the perspective was out of whack. What he

Sylbert drenched storefronts on the Universal backlot in Dick Tracy *colors.*

had envisioned as a series of narrow marble arches looked more like an arch and a half, and the corridor was barely half the length it was supposed to be. With the carpenters, Sylbert and Harold Michelson went to work redesigning the set right on the spot, eyeballing the arches into place and mounting several of them on marble columns to create a forced perspective, an optical illusion that made the hallway look much longer than it actually was.

The Club Ritz.

With Sylbert's art direction and Storaro's lighting, the front steps of Tess Trueheart's street sparkled with fairy-tale magic.

Throughout this hectic preproduction period, transportation coordinator Joel Marrow crisscrossed the country on a two-month sojourn in search of the "generic" cars Warren Beatty had envisioned for the film. Shopping through periodicals advertising classic and antique cars, Marrow zeroed in on models manufactured between 1935 and 1939. The cars from those years had a basic similarity in design. He compiled a notebook with five hundred pictures of different cars, eventually winnowing the selection down to half a dozen models that he could show to Beatty and Sylbert so they could make their choices for each of the cars in the movie.

The police cars were all modified '36 Fords. Tracy drove a made-over Ford five-window coupe. The gangsters, who had flashier tastes in wheels, drove Chryslers or Chevys with their hood ornaments, grilles, and hubcaps customized for the film. Big Boy got chauffeured around the city in a '38 Cadillac limousine, which Marrow's staff retooled so it could be identified only as "the biggest, bluest car anybody had ever seen." Breathless Mahoney got the flashiest car of all. After deliberating over the sexy cars of the era, the *Dick Tracy* brain trust selected an Auburn bobtail speedster for the film's *femme fatale*.

Not all of the cars were in good condition, so Marrow and crew went over them from bumper-to-bumper, replacing parts and engines, getting the gauges to work, and replacing windshields and windows that had smoked-over with age. In addition, the cars that would be used in the stunts had to be outfitted with modern engines and transmissions to give them the power the stuntmen needed to operate within the margins of safety.

Once production began, the "closed set" occasionally had visitors, whose appreciation of the production design encouraged Sylbert. Barbra Streisand came out to visit Beatty one day when he was shooting a scene in Mumbles' hotel room.

"It was this little room, and because Dick Tracy's going to come into it, it's got Dick Tracy Yellow. Pat was with Dick Tracy, so it's got the green, and Mumbles was dressed in fuchsia, and all his fuchsia clothes were hanging in frame. Barbra stood right next to me. And there's nothing in this damn room! I mean, there's color on the wall, and there's a little old wooden dresser with a circular mirror that we painted yellow, the door was yellow with green panels, so when the yellow guy and the green guy come in, the door is right there, framing them. And she said, 'It is *so beautiful*.'" Sylbert shrugged. "It was a *wall!* But that was the effect it had on people."

The hotel lobby, as envisioned by Sylbert. The rough pencil sketch worked out the dimensions of the scene.

Bill Major's production illustration of the hotel lobby.

The hotel lobby as realized in the film.

Sylbert and Michelson had to eyeball the forced perspective in this City Hall corridor to create the illusion of depth. The set was only twenty-five feet long.

So there was beauty in the design, and there was deceptive depth as well. The limited palette of colors and the squared-off style were neither as limited nor as square as they appeared on the drawing boards—because before a scene went on film, Vittorio Storaro gave it a bath of shadow and light. The fact that ninety percent of the story takes place at night meant that Storaro's lighting could shape and color the film further, in effect picking up the design work where Sylbert and Canonero left off. The primary colors of Canonero's costumes moved in and out of the light; energy forces colliding in the night. Thick black shadows danced on the bare walls of Sylbert's sets, adding depth and mystery to every scene. Storaro's specialized technique for processing exposed film, called ENR, meant that he could make the blacks extremely saturated, thus eliminating the graininess and vulgarity that frequently plague films shot in such a half-light style.

They pushed the design elements of the movies as far as they could while trying to maintain the gossamer believability of life in Chester Gould's skewed universe. The balance between Light and Darkness, between the Beautiful Faces and the Grotesque, between a Real City and a Cartoon City—these were the parameters of the Dick Tracy mythology. Too much weighty realism and it would never fly; too much airy fantasy and it would float away. The proper dynamic was somewhere between the two, and Sylbert, for one, felt that production design was not the deciding factor in keeping it there: "The prosthetics and the mattes were more important than anything else. The picture wouldn't be *Dick Tracy* if the mattes and prosthetics didn't work. It had nothing to do with dialogue. It had nothing to do with lighting. It had nothing to do with sets. It's mattes and prosthetics you're watching with the most care—to not go over the line, and yet make them human and believable."

For Richard Sylbert, seeing his designs come to life in the hands of such talented and savvy professionals (not to mention friends) as Warren Beatty, Milena Canonero, and Vittorio Storaro was only a percentage of the thrill of doing the movie. The real thrill came with getting scared again, walking the high wire without a net, reconnoitering without a compass.

"There are some filmmakers, very talented people, of whom I like to say the only thing they lack is inexperience. *All* they have is experience. You can learn most of what there is to know in the movie business in about an hour—you've got four lenses, this thing has wheels . . . know what I'm saying? The beauty of this movie was that we consciously got rid of our past, and put ourselves in a position where we had to learn. The great fun of this picture was that it was a great time in my life to take this kind of risk."

With his work on *Dick Tracy* completed, Sylbert talked like a man who had not only found his way home without a compass, but had discovered gold along the way. He had been nominated for six Academy Awards, winning for *Who's Afraid of Virginia Woolf?*, but none of it compared to the adventurous outing on *Dick Tracy*.

"This picture is the only picture in my opinion that anybody should be really be proud of. For Milena, Vittorio, and myself to pat ourselves on the back for doing the other movies that we've done so many times, so successfully, it's stupid. This picture, you say to yourself, this was worth doing. It was worth doing because you couldn't rest for a minute. In a normal movie, you rent the palace in Peking, what're you going to tell me about it? But you couldn't do that here. You couldn't do rent-a-palace, you couldn't do rent-a-city. Nothing was free."

Richard Sylbert didn't set out to create a beautiful or sophisticated production design. He tried to make it simple. In doing so, he created a design which, in its flawless perfection, became beautiful, in its many applications, became sophisticated. The placid surface of the picture belies its turbulent depths, where monsters, and the stuff of myths, await.

Perhaps the ultimate beauty of *Dick Tracy*'s design can be described by the way in which its apparent limitations actually freed the film's creators to imagine a whole new world. As an orchestration of filmmaking talent, it called for virtuosity, balance, and harmony, and an understanding of storytelling dynamics. The design of *Dick Tracy* never hit a false note. This came as no surprise to Richard Sylbert, who, after all, doesn't work with hummers.

Diopter shot of graveyard in **Dick Tracy**. *The effect added a dash of Hitchcock to the film.*

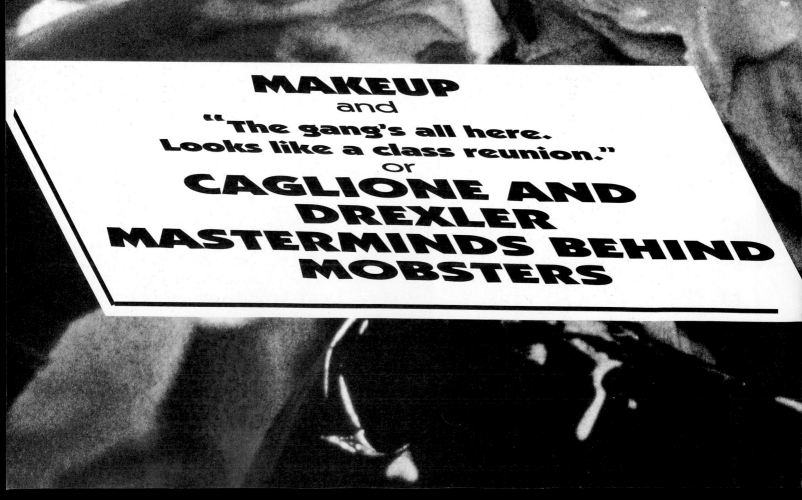

MAKEUP
and
"The gang's all here.
Looks like a class reunion."
or
CAGLIONE AND
DREXLER
MASTERMINDS BEHIND
MOBSTERS

The Kid, who has been around the block a time or two, dodges the cops, McGillicuddy and Ives, and finds himself inside the Seventh Street Garage. At a table inside the garage, five men sit playing stud poker—Little Face, The Brow, Shoulders, Stooge, and The Rodent. The Kid's eyes widen and so do ours. These faces are new to the movies. What kind of world is this? What forces have shaped the grotesque physiognomies of these creatures? Suddenly, Flattop bursts into the garage, submachine gun blazing. At this point we don't have a choice. We need to see more.

Caglione and Drexler—remember the names. These two guys make faces for a living. Faces you can't forget. With their extraordinary prosthetic makeup appliances, John Caglione and Doug Drexler brought Chester Gould's abominable villains to life with a conviction that breathes believability into every frame of *Dick Tracy.*

Working primarily on the East Coast, Caglione and Drexler had already amassed an impressive list of credits—*Altered States, Zelig, FX, Making Mr. Right,* and *The Cotton Club,* to name a few—when Milena Canonero, the costume designer on *Cotton Club* insisted that Warren Beatty interview them for *Dick Tracy.* It was a long shot. Every makeup jockey in the motion picture business was going after the *Tracy* gig.

As protégés of makeup artist Dick Smith—who had revolutionized the use of foam-latex appliances in his work on such films as *The Exorcist, Little Big Man,* and *The Godfather*—Caglione and Drexler specialized in the kind of characters Beatty was looking for. It was a match made in makeup heaven, "the cream job of all time," as Drexler described it.

Like scientists who, independent of one another, make identical discoveries in their labs, Caglione and Drexler had learned separately of the miracles of illusion that could be created with foam-latex appliances. Each had sought out and struck up a friendship with the aforementioned Dick Smith. It was Smith who eventually introduced them. When they finally met, they felt like long-lost brothers, both of whom had makeup in their blood.

John Caglione always had a fascination with monsters. As a youngster, he eagerly ogled all the old Universal horror films, the Frankensteins, werewolves,

The first step in the creation of an appliance was to take an impression of the actor's face with a substance called alginate.

Itchy, Big Boy, Flattop, Numbers, and Influence hold court at the Club Ritz.

and ghouls who were the handiwork of a makeup man named Jack Pierce. Caglione's interest in the monster-making process led him to take up makeup as a hobby. And so, at an age when most boys are more interested in curve balls and carburetors, Caglione was figuring out how to make people look like lagoon creatures.

Among his junior-high classmates in Troy, New York, Caglione's hobby earned him the nickname Maybelline Boy, but that didn't stop him from devouring all he could on the subject. And when, at the age of thirteen, he saw *The Exorcist*, the extraordinary creations of makeup artist Dick Smith had such a powerful impact on Caglione that he knew he had found his calling.

"I remember seeing that movie and sleeping in my parents' bedroom for two weeks. It really affected me, really scared me," recalled Caglione. "And then I worked up the courage to write a letter to Dick Smith. I didn't have his address, but I had this Rona Barrett magazine that said if you wanted to write a letter to the Linda Blair Fan Club you wrote to Warner Brothers Studios in Hollywood. I was hopeful that Dick Smith lived in Hollywood, and in some way that letter might get to him. And some very nice person at Warner's forwarded

Paul Sorvino as oyster-eater Lips Manlis.

that letter to Dick Smith in Larchmont, New York. So at thirteen years old, I got a handwritten reply from Dick Smith saying he wanted to see my work, and to send him photographs, and I started a friendship with him that has lasted seventeen years now. He really got the ball rolling for me.

"I went to his house to meet him and I was raving about his Linda Blair makeup, going 'Yeah, that's great, she was so scary!' and he asked what I thought of Father Merrin, the old priest. I said, well, he was a nice old guy. And he said 'That whole thing was a rubber makeup, here, let me show you. . . .' And he started pulling out these pieces. He had Max Von Sydow's life cast, and he pulled out the jowls and the neck appliance, and *it was Father Merrin!* And at that moment, standing there with Dick Smith, seeing those appliances on Max Von Sydow, that's when I decided *I have to do this,* I have to sit down and reevaluate my life, because this is something that I really want bad. And I don't know why, I guess because it's self-expression, something that comes from within."

With a recommendation from Smith, Caglione got a staff job at NBC in New York at age eighteen, and was

soon concocting coneheads and killer bees for "Saturday Night Live." The rest, as film historians will someday say, is makeup history.

When you reach the answering machine at Caglione and Drexler's lab in Los Angeles, John answers the phone:

"This is John, of Caglione and Drexler. Doug and I are in the middle of a very dangerous experiment. Please leave a message and we'll call you right back. . . . " (In the background, Doug shouts in alarm. John wails into the phone and then . . . instead of a bang there's a beep.)

Caglione and Drexler have fun with their work. It was their tonic for the killer hours and sometimes intense pressure of *Dick Tracy.* The pressure of getting hundreds of pieces of latex glued to faces that would contort, perspire, and eat fried chicken for twelve hours, and if any one of those hundreds of pieces, some with edges as fine as butterfly wings, misbehaved, they wouldn't be doing their job. They had to laugh. It meant keeping their sanity.

"Every time you do a makeup it's a performance,"

Caglione and Drexler saw something in actor Chuck Hicks's forehead that told them it would look right with a piece of latex glued to it.

The Brow played by Chuck Hicks.

The Brow.

The original version of The Brow.

noted Drexler. "It's physically and mentally taxing. It takes extraordinary, heavy-duty concentration for hours on end at godawful hours—like 3 A.M.—hours before anyone else gets to the set. The appliances have to laid onto the actor's face perfectly. You can't miss. If you lay it down a little bit too far to the left, when he smiles, you're going to get wrinkles running across his face in an unnatural way. Plus, when an appliance goes down, you've got to apply a certain amount of tension as you're gluing it, or the wrinkles will run the wrong way. All these things add up to a lot of tension in the morning before we shoot. John and I have a camaraderie that keeps it relaxed and makes it fun. And if one guy gets bent out of shape, he brings the other guy back to earth."

Doug Drexler's laugh is infectious. It's the laugh of a man in love with latex. While Caglione knew that there was face paint in his future, Drexler went ape over it later in life.

He was working his way toward a career as an illustrator in New York City. "Like John, I've always been fantasy-oriented, and drawing was the best way for a little kid to explore all kinds of worlds. There's no limit

Steve the Tramp had a prosthetic jawbone that jutted out four inches from Tony Epper's own.

to what you can do on a piece of paper. You can go anywhere. Thinking is the best way to travel," he enthused.

One Halloween, Drexler discovered basic instructions in an old science-fiction magazine for making a latex character makeup, and baked up a *Planet of the Apes* face in his oven at home. Intrigued by the artistic possibilities and the simplicity of the process, he was soon reading everything he could on the craft. It was, he explained, "as if a genetic switch had been thrown. It had taken me by the collar and wouldn't let me go." Soon he, too, was paying a visit to Dick Smith.

To visualize Steve the Tramp, Caglione imagined a history of the character, including the cauliflowered-eared legacy of a thousand waterfront brawls.

Maquette *for Steve the Tramp.*   *Cag 'n' Drex drawing of Steve the Tramp .*

Drexler quit his job of four years to work with Smith for two weeks on *The Hunger* ("No contest.") and ended up staying on for the entire film. *"The Hunger* was the ultimate school," he said. "David Bowie ages to over a hundred years old, there's puppets, there's mummy suits . . . it was just after that, on my second job, that I met John."

The job was *Amityville III.* ("We don't even know why they made *Two,*" Drexler said with a laugh, "but we weren't going to argue.") They became partners and set up their first lab in the basement of Caglione's home in Floral Park, New York. "John's wife, Helen, was trying to run a home with kids and everything, and we were down there with plaster and clay, and also being wild sometimes and having water fights and screaming."

Working with Canonero and production designer Richard Sylbert on *The Cotton Club* provided the entrée to Warren Beatty and the *Dick Tracy* project. They had made a name for themselves in the East, but in Hollywood they were still neophytes, and they were nervous about meeting Beatty for the first time. "We waited for forty-five minutes in the screening room in his home," remembered Drexler. "And he comes bounding down the stairs soaking wet in a towel and says, 'What can we do?' And we said 'You mean about the makeup?' And he said, 'The story, the script—what can we do to make it better?' And this blew our minds. We had never been asked that question before by a director or producer or anything. Nobody usually cared. We spent most of the time talking about the script, what we thought could make it better, what we found interesting."

When they learned they had the job, there were working on a TV-movie in Montreal. The phone in

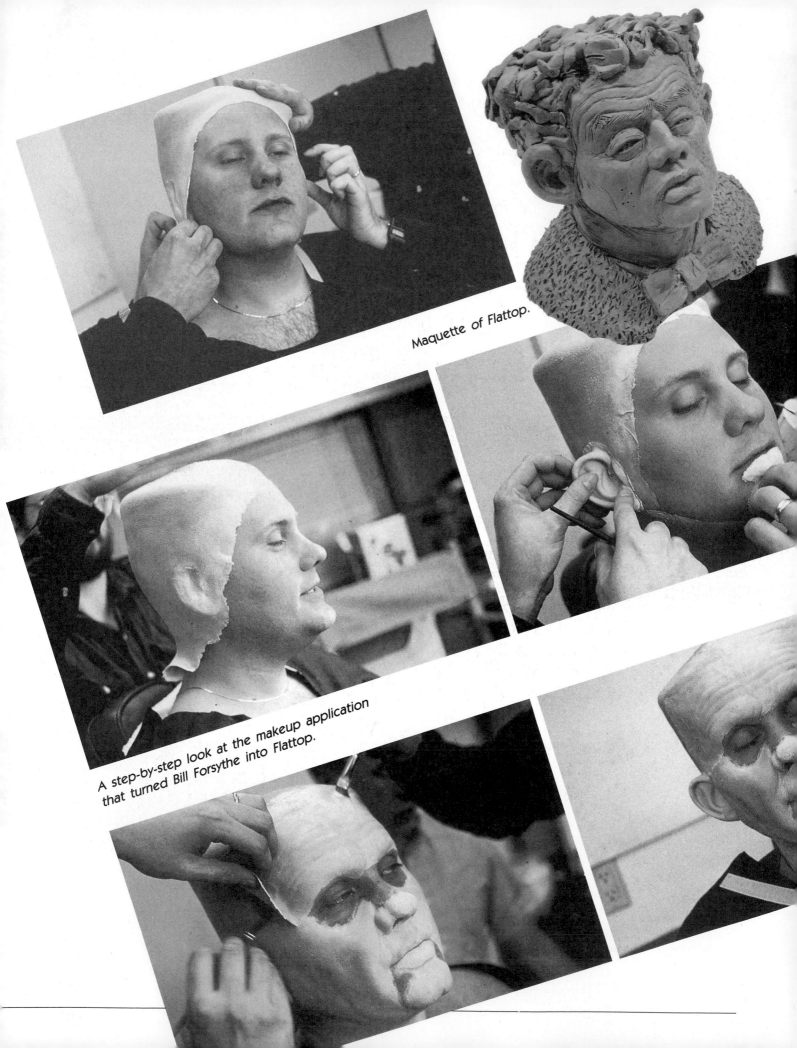

Maquette of Flattop.

A step-by-step look at the makeup application that turned Bill Forsythe into Flattop.

AND ME—THEY JUST CALL ME FLATTOP.

Chester Gould's original Flattop. When Gould killed him off, mournful fans staged a mock funeral.

Caglione's hotel room rang at 2:30 A.M. It was *Dick Tracy* production manager Jon Landau calling with the good news. Caglione burst into Drexler's room so excitedly that his partner thought there was a fire. They spent five minutes bouncing up and down on the beds. The two face-aces had gotten the most sought-after makeup job of the year. *Dick Tracy* was theirs!

In September of 1988, "Cag 'n' Drex" moved to L.A. and lived out of suitcases while building a makeup lab from square one in a Van Nuys, California, industrial park.

Influence, as he appeared in the original comics.

As a first step in creating the *Tracy* makeups, they sketched character faces that were more rounded and three-dimensional looking than the Chester Gould cartoons. This was their way of appraising the character's features to see what would work, practically speaking, and what wouldn't.

They next sculpted *maquettes,* small preliminary clay models that were shown to the key creative people on the film for comment and critique. "We didn't want the picture to get too far into Toon Land," reflected Caglione. "You couldn't have half the charac-

ters walking around looking like real monsters, and the other half not. You'd lose the audience. We had to split the difference between reality and fantasy. I made them realize that we could do Flattop, but we didn't have to make him exactly like the comic strip. Just a half a turn of the screw into fantasy, just a kick. That's it, no farther. If you go any farther, then Warren looks out of place next to Flattop, and Flattop looks out of place next to Madonna."

Caglione and Drexler were directly involved in the selection of the film's bad guys. An open casting call

Maquette of Influence.

Influence. "This guy could look at you for ten seconds and he'd own you," said actor Henry Silva of his character.

Caglione (l.) and Drexler (r.) turn Neil Summers into The Rodent.

The Rodent, as imagined by Chester Gould.

Neil Summers, The Rodent.

brought a virtual convention of character actors to the Hollywood Methodist Church, where the makeup men shot hundreds of Polaroids in their search for the faces that would become the basis for their prosthetics. They weren't tied down to a particular group of villains. Beatty told them if there were any of Gould's ghoulies in particular that they'd like to create, they should feel free. The names in the script would simply be replaced.

On some of the characters, the actor's face was almost completely concealed by latex appliances. There was very little of Tony Epper's face in Steve the Tramp, for instance. For the other villains, Caglione and Drexler helped cast actors whose appearance gave them a head start toward the character. "We tried to find someone who was on their way to being that character," Drexler observed. "Even if it was just ten percent, or if it was just their eyes. Something to build from, so that it was not an entirely fabricated person.

"We thought Ed O'Ross had some of Itchy in his facial structure already, so we thought that he was a perfect Itchy. R. G. Armstrong, who plays Pruneface—the minute we saw him, we thought we could give him seventy percent more of what he already had. Neil Summers, who played The Rodent—Neil was kind of on his way to being The Rodent anyway. We couldn't pass him up.

And with Bill Forsythe, there was something in the eyes that suggested Flattop."

With the actors cast, the actual creation of the makeup appliances began. Caglione described the process step-by-step:

"We get the actor in and sit him in the chair and put a bald cap on him to block his own hair out. Then we take prosthetic impression material—it's the same stuff the dentist uses to take impressions inside your mouth, that gelatinous material, it's called alginate. We mix it fast in bowls because it sets in four minutes. We put this stuff all over the actor's head, and when it sets it turns into this Jell-O-like material that we reinforce with plaster-of-paris. When we take it off, we have an impression of the actor's face.

"We pour plaster into the alginate impression, and when the plaster hardens, we peel off the alginate and we have a cast of the actor's face. A life mask. Every pore and every wrinkle show up in this cast.

"We put the life mask on the sculpting stand and start attaching the clay and sculpting the character's face. After the sculpture has been approved, we take an X-Acto blade and cut into the clay sculpture where we want each appliance to meet the next appliance. Dick Smith came up with this technique. In the old days,

"Ears looking at you." A table full of extra ears fresh from the oven.

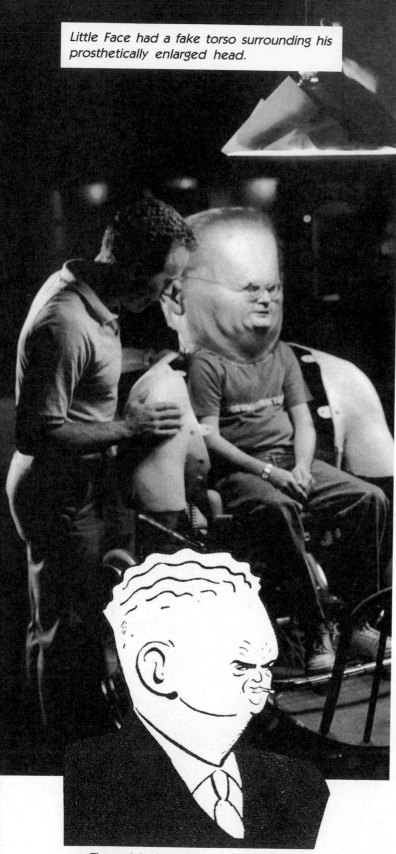

Little Face had a fake torso surrounding his prosthetically enlarged head.

The original version of Little Face.

when they did an elaborate foam-latex makeup, they made one big mask, which made it impossible to glue every bit of it down. Separate pieces tend to fit more naturally on the face than a whole big piece of foam glued to your head.

"Then we make positive and negative molds of each clay piece. The molds are made out of a material called Ultracol. We clean the clay out of the molds and put them back together with wet foam in there, and we stick it in the oven for about three hours until it bakes. When we take it out and take it apart there's a fully cured foam-latex appliance."

These latex pieces aren't reusable, so Caglione and Drexler's staff had to fashion a fresh batch of appliances for every day of filming. At times, they had as many as twenty-five people working as artists and lab technicians, including some of the top young makeup experts in the business, such as Vee Neal (who won an Oscar for her work on *Beetlejuice*), Kevin Haney, and Craig Riordan.

The first two performers to come out of makeup as *Dick Tracy* characters were Tony Epper as Steve the Tramp and Bill Forsythe as Flattop.

Caglione outlined the sordid background of Steve the Tramp: "He gets into fights every Friday night for money, he beats up the Kid, he's a skid-row bum, he's weatherbeaten—all those things are good for the makeup person to keep in mind when he's sculpting. Steve's whole head was rubber. He wore cauliflower ears, a lot of deep wrinkles, a really gnarly forehead, deep-socketed eyes, and this big old shovel jaw that was about four inches off Tony Epper's real chin."

Epper's jaw was so far off the chin, in fact, that Caglione had to urge him to exaggerate his facial movements. "I told him that he really had to eat that chicken, let his lips roam around his face, because what he did one-hundred percent on the inside, we were only seeing thirty percent on the outside," said Caglione.

The appliances on Bill Forsythe were much thinner—some pieces were less than an eighth of an inch thick—which meant a greater range of movement. The fourteen separate pieces used to create the face made Flattop the most complex prosthetic job in the picture. According to Drexler, "No one else had it as bad as he did. I think he drew from this as a source for the anger he displayed as Flattop. It shone like a beacon. Something that you could not act."

Ed O'Ross thoroughly researched his role as Itchy. He made volumes of background notes about the character, which he pinned next to comic-strip drawings of Itchy on the wall in his study at home. O'Ross also phoned *Dick Tracy* buffs around the U.S. to get as much background information as he could about Itchy. As a result, when he got the makeup put on for the first time, "he was ready," Drexler remarked. "When he stood up from the makeup chair, he *was* Itchy."

The makeup department manufactured hundreds of spare facial parts—a "bag of tricks," Beatty took to calling it—that could be used to jazz up the appearance of the film's background characters. It was out of this bag of tricks that the two of them helped Al Pacino ferret out the features and character of Big Boy.

As drawn by Chester Gould, Big Boy looked nothing

like Al Pacino. The character in the movie was wholly Pacino's inspiration. "Al wanted to play Mister Potato Head," recalled Drexler. "He wanted to try on a lot of things, and the makeup would grow from one piece. He'd find a nose out of the hundreds of noses that we had, and there'd be something about it—he didn't know what it was—he'd sit in the chair in front of the mirror and hold the nose in place and the character would grow from that in his mind. And then John sculpted the final design for Big Boy based upon all the pieces that we'd mixed and matched together."

"When I met Al, I was really nervous," Caglione added, "because I love his work. I loved the *Godfa-*

The negative impression made by the alginate was then used to create a "life mask," a perfect plaster reproduction of the actor's face.

thers. He said to me, 'We're going to create a character together, aren't we?' Really enthusiastic. Yeah? He'd look over my shoulder while I was sculpting on his life mask and we'd talk about the character. He worked on the body posture, the speech pattern, and the walk. In about a week and a half he had it nailed."

When Pacino arrived the morning of a shooting day for his Big Boy makeup, Caglione and Drexler witnessed an amazing transformation. "It was really funny, because he'd come in as Al, and sit down in the chair, and we'd start putting the makeup on," said Drexler. "He would doze off in the chair. And always at the same point, just as we were putting the first color on the appliances, he'd wake up a little bit and just kind of roll his eyes toward the ceiling and smack his lips a little bit, then doze back off. But once the makeup was finished, he'd wake up again *completely disoriented.* It was like Al's consciousness had been lifted out of his head and Big Boy had been put in there! He didn't know where he was, he didn't know who we were, he'd be like (as Big Boy) 'Who are you guys? What's goin' on?' He was Big Boy for the rest of the day—always crazy, always nutty, always offered you walnuts."

Caglione worried incessantly about Pacino's makeup staying on. "I've never seen makeup come off an actor's face so fast," he remarked. "He's really an explosive, dynamic actor. He's aware of makeup being on his face, but he's not intimidated by it at all. And his character is a live wire. I'd be there on the set holding my breath, waiting for his chin to pop off onto the table!" Caglione marveled at the memory of working

Pruneface, played by R. G. Armstrong.

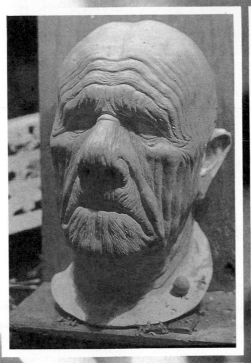

A clay image of the character face got sculpted over the actor's life mask. This shot shows the Pruneface sculpture over the R. G. Armstrong life mask. The artists used an X-Acto blade to cut the clay sculpture into separate pieces, and each piece was placed on its own individual mold.

Pruneface, as drawn by Gould.

Drexler (in foreground) and Caglione touch up Pruneface on the Dick Tracy set. The film was "the cream job of all time" for the two young makeup artists.

with one of his idols. "That was a great experience for us, to work with him and develop a character with him."

Dick Tracy yielded one great experience after another for the makeup artists. One of these was the creation of the makeup for the actor who played Mumbles. Said Caglione: "We were all nervous, because the makeup hadn't been tested, we'd only had five days to get it ready, and it was going before the camera that day. We had no idea how it was going to work. He had these lips that were twisted over to one side, and he had brow covers and a bald scalp and a blond wig. He looked in the mirror and told us that if we'd had any more time we would've screwed it up—which was a great compliment. We were on cloud nine. He looked in the mirror and loved it, and he just ran with it. We'd never worked with these high-caliber actors before, and we saw them do magic."

To make sure the illusion held up in front of the camera, Caglione had intensive talks with director of photography Vittorio Storaro. Prosthetic makeups cannot be lit like human skin. There's no blood and fascia. The foam latex doesn't radiate warmth. What sells the reality of the appliance on an actor's face are the colors used to paint it—the reds, the beard shadow, the freckles, moles, and veins which convince the viewer that it's flesh. The wrong color lighting will literally wash away the illusion.

So to safeguard the makeup's payload of illusion, Storaro built a special lighting device so that Caglione and Drexler could test the colors of their paint palette. "We tweaked our colors, Vittorio tweaked his lighting a little bit and that was it," said Caglione.

Both the makeup artists felt that their background as New Yorkers helped them add the value of reality to their *Dick Tracy* creations. When he worked at NBC,

Caglione (l.) and Drexler (r.) apply an alginate mask to the face of the Unknown Actor.

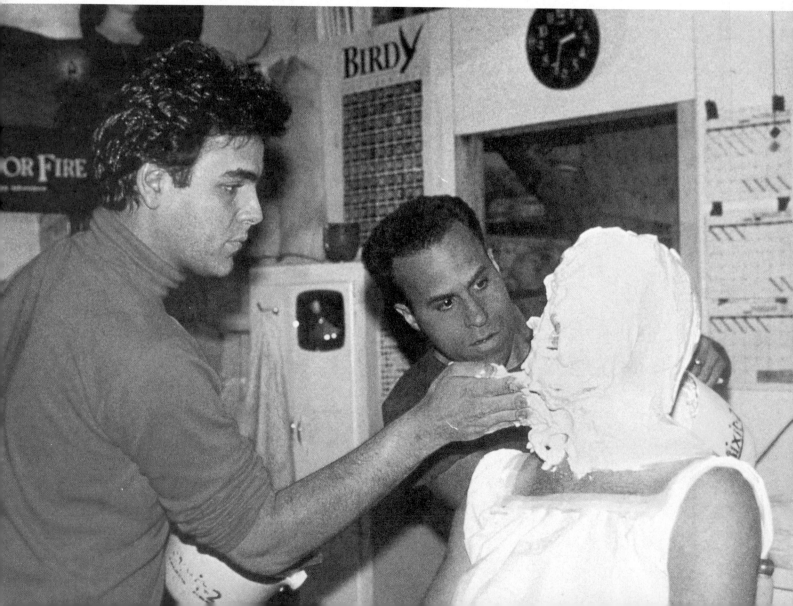

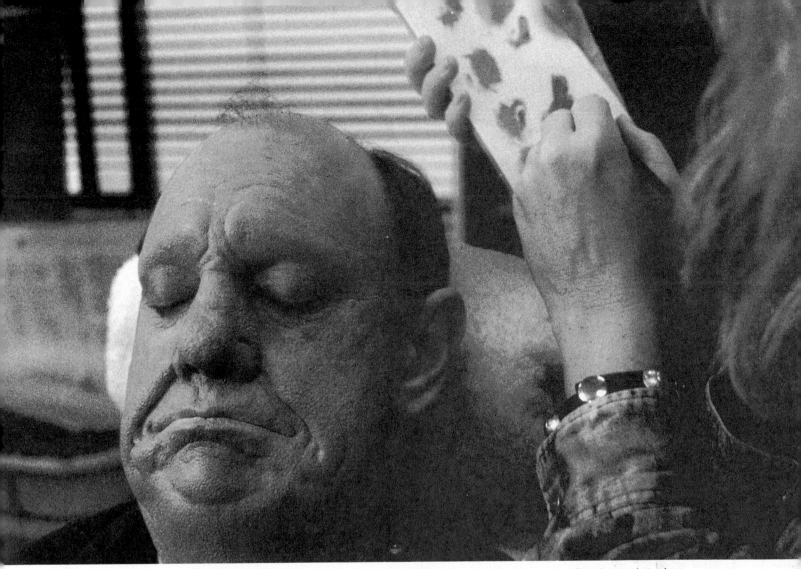

Jim Wilkey, on his way to becoming Edward "Stooge" Barnes, gets his latex appliances painted.

Caglione rode the New York City subway—the Fort Knox of faces—to Rockefeller Center everyday. He did makeup for the local NBC affiliate's "Live at Five" guests and, again, had the chance to study thousands of faces.

Mused Drexler: "In L.A., everyone is so smooth and beautiful. I really can't get over it sometimes. But in New York, the faces are full of character, the craggy faces, the real nitty gritty, the Chester Gould types. It's an education in human faces and the incredible array of characters."

Being New Yorkers, they (surprise, surprise) spoke their minds. "I think Warren appreciated that, and he knew that we were going to lay it on the line every time," Drexler asserted. "And we did. Warren takes risks. He's an innovator. He took a chance on us. I thought it was a big one, really."

"I'd never felt like we were *on* a picture before like we were *on* this one," concluded Caglione. "It was great. I remember our first few weeks. . . . First of all, I couldn't believe we got the job. That fried my brain. And I'd be sitting in meetings, and there's Milena Canonero there, and there's Richard Sylbert, and Vittorio Storaro, and Warren Beatty! And I'm saying to myself, What am I doing here? What's going on? But they made us feel very comfortable. We had a lot of great allies. We miss it. We can't wait for the sequel."